Introduction to the Philosophy of Education

By the same author

The Educational Philosophy of National Socialism (Yale)
The Education of the Mexican Nation (Columbia)
Higher Learning in Britain (California)
Existentialism and Education (Wiley, 1964)
Introduction to the Philosophy of Education (Wiley, 1964)
The Art and Science of Creativity (Holt)
Educational Anthropology (Wiley, 1965)
Logic and Languages of Education (Wiley, 1966)
Education and Economic Thought (Wiley, 1968)
Foundations of Education, Third Edition (Wiley, 1971)
Science in Education (Wiley, 1972)

INTRODUCTION TO THE PHILOSOPHY OF EDUCATION

Second Edition

George F. Kneller

University of California, Los Angeles

John Wiley & Sons, Inc.

New York · London · Sydney · Toronto

Library of Congress Catalogue Card Number: 78-168637
ISBN 0-471-49512-3 (cloth)
ISBN 0-471-49515-8 (paper)

Printed in the United States of America

10 9 8 7 6 5 4 3

Preface

Although much has been written in the past few years on the proper nature of educational philosophy, I have not been convinced of a need to change my own point of view. Briefly, I consider educational philosophy, like social and political philosophy, to be a branch of formal philosophy, modified, as I illustrate in this book, by ideas emerging from all realms of the educational enterprise. I also adopt the systematic (in contrast to the analytic) approach. Whereas the analyst breaks concepts down, and I do some of this myself, I prefer to put them back together again. I value the work of the analyst and consider it indispensable, but I value synthesis more highly, believing it to be the ultimate ideal, especially in an age of almost rampant specialization.

In this second edition, I lay greater stress on matters of knowledge and value and somewhat lesser stress on the formal categories of philosophy. I do so largely in response to the increased attention now being paid to problems of personal as well as cognitive knowledge and to the human as well as academic value of what is learned. Reflecting a heightened interest everywhere in new modes of philosophizing, I assign separate chapters to existentialism and analysis. I have enriched the content of the former by drawing upon the writings of existentialists themselves, but only in those relatively few instances where they reflect upon education in existential fashion. The new chapter on analysis moves away from a concentration on logical empiricism into applications of logic, language, and analysis. Here I have added two short analyses of my own—on "equality" and on "teaching."

As in the case of the first edition, this work is a compilation of chapters written originally for a text I edited entitled *Foundations of Education* (Wiley, 1971). My purpose remains the same: to provide institutions of teacher education with a book that will summarize the subject within the time normally available. Although the study of educational philosophy has become more widespread during the past decade, America's colleges and universities on the whole still lag behind their European counterparts in emphasizing the profound contribution that philosophy can make toward an understanding of education. I hope that this book will in some small way help to remedy the situation.

George F. Kneller

University of California
Los Angeles
April, 1971

Contents

Introduction to the Philosophy of Education

1

The Relevance of Philosophy

From time to time every teacher and student asks himself questions that are implicitly philosophical. The teacher wonders, "Why am I teaching? Why am I teaching history? What is teaching at its best?" And the student asks, "Why am I studying algebra? What am I going to school for anyway?" Taken far enough, these questions become philosophical. They become questions about the nature of man and the world, about knowledge, value, and the good life.

MODES OF PHILOSOPHY

Unfortunately, nothing illuminating can be said about philosophy with a single definition. Let us therefore think of philosophy as an activity in three modes or styles: the speculative, the prescriptive, and the analytic.

1

Speculative Philosophy. Speculative philosophy is a way of thinking systematically about everything that exists. Why do philosophers want to do this? Why are they not content, like scientists, to study particular aspects of reality? The answer is that the human mind wishes to see things as a whole. It wishes to understand how all the different things that have been discovered together form some sort of meaningful totality. We are all aware of this tendency in ourselves. When we read a book, look at a painting, or study an assignment, we are concerned not only with particular details but also with the order or pattern that gives these details their significance. Speculative philosophy, then, is a search for order and wholeness, applied not to particular items or experiences but to all knowledge and all experience. In brief, speculative philosophy is the attempt to find a coherence in the whole realm of thought and experience.

Prescriptive Philosophy. Prescriptive philosophy seeks to establish standards for assessing values, judging conduct, and appraising art. It examines what we mean by good and bad, right and wrong, beautiful and ugly. It asks whether these qualities inhere in things themselves or whether they are projections of our own minds. To the experimental psychologist the varieties of human conduct are morally neither good nor bad; they are simply forms of behavior to be studied empirically. But to the educator and the prescriptive philosopher some forms of behavior are worthwhile and others are not. The prescriptive philosopher seeks to discover and to recommend principles for deciding what actions and qualities are most worthwhile and why they should be so.

Analytic Philosophy. Analytic philosophy focuses on words and meaning. The analytic philosopher examines such notions as "cause," "mind," "academic freedom," and "equality of opportunity" in order to assess the different meanings they carry in different contexts. He shows how inconsistencies may arise when meanings appropriate in certain contexts are imported into others. The analytic philosopher tends to be skeptical, cautious, and disinclined to build systems of thought.

Today the analytic approach dominates American and British philosophy. On the Continent the speculative tradition prevails. But whichever approach is uppermost at any time, most philosophers agree that all approaches contribute to the health of philosophy. Speculation unaccompanied by analysis soars too easily into a heaven of its own, irrelevant to the world as we know it; analysis without speculation descends to minutiae and becomes sterile. In any case few philosophers are solely speculative, solely prescriptive, or solely analytic. Speculation, prescription, and analysis are all present to some degree in the work of all mature philosophers.

PHILOSOPHY AND SCIENCE

A great deal of information has been gathered by various sciences on subjects treated by philosophy, particularly human nature. But when we look at this information, we find that psychology gives us one picture of man, sociology another, biology another, and so on. What we have after all the sciences have been searched is not a composite picture of man but a series of different pictures. These pictures fail to satisfy because they explain different aspects of man rather than man as a whole. Can we unify our partial pictures of man into one that is single and complete? Yes, but not by using scientific methods alone. It is through philosophy that we unify the separate findings of science and interrelate the fundamental concepts these findings presuppose.

The philosopher considers questions that arise before and after the scientist has done his work. Traditional science presupposes, for example, that every event is caused by other events and in turn causes still other events. Hence, for science no event is uncaused. But how can we be sure of this? Do cause and effect exist in the world itself or are they read into the world by men? These questions cannot be answered scientifically because causality is not a finding but an assumption of science. Unless the scientist assumes that reality is causal in nature, he cannot begin to investigate it. Again, science deals with things as they appear to our senses and to our instruments. But are things in themselves really the same as they appear to us? The scientist cannot say, because things in themselves, as opposed to their appearances, are by definition beyond empirical verification.

Philosophy, then, is both natural and necessary to man. We are forever seeking some comprehensive framework within which our separate findings may be given a total significance. Not only is philosophy a branch of knowledge along with art, science, and history, but also it actually embraces these disciplines in their theoretical reaches and seeks to establish connections between them. Once again, *philosophy attempts to establish a coherence throughout the whole domain of experience.*

PHILOSOPHY OF EDUCATION

Beside having its own concerns, philosophy considers the fundamental assumptions of other branches of knowledge. When philosophy turns its attention to science, we have philosophy of science; when it examines the basic concepts of the law, we have philosophy of law; and when it deals with education, we have philosophy of education or educational philosophy.

Just as formal philosophy attempts to understand reality as a whole by explaining it in the most general and systematic way, so educational philosophy seeks to comprehend education in its entirety, interpreting it by means of general concepts that will guide our choice of educational ends and policies. In the same way that general philosophy coordinates the findings of the different sciences, educational philosophy interprets these findings as they bear on education. Scientific theories do not carry direct educational implications; they cannot be applied to educational practice without first being examined philosophically.

Educational philosophy depends on general or formal philosophy to the extent that the problems of education are of a general philosophical character. We cannot criticize existing educational policies or suggest new ones without considering such general philosophic problems as (a) the nature of the good life, to which education should lead; (b) the nature of man himself, because it is man we are educating; (c) the nature of society, because education is a social process; and (d) the nature of ultimate reality, which all knowledge seeks to penetrate. Educational philosophy, then, involves among other things the application of formal philosophy to the field of education.[1]

Like general philosophy, educational philosophy is speculative, prescriptive, and analytic. It is speculative when it seeks to establish theories of the nature of man, society, and the world by which to order and interpret the conflicting data of educational research and the behavioral sciences. It is prescriptive when it specifies the ends that education ought to follow and the general means it should use to attain them. It is analytic when it clarifies speculative and prescriptive statements. The analyst, as we shall see, examines the rationality of our educational ideas, their consistency with other ideas, and the ways in which they are distorted by loose thinking. He tests the logic of our concepts and their inadequacy to the facts they seek to explain. Above all, he attempts to clarify the many different meanings that have been attached to such heavily worked educational terms as "freedom," "adjustment," "growth," "experience," "needs," and "knowledge."

We are now ready to consider the various branches of philosophy, particularly metaphysics, as they relate to education.

THE NATURE OF REALITY

Metaphysics is mainly the province of speculative philosophy. Its central concern is the nature of ultimate reality. Metaphysics seeks to answer such questions as these: Does the universe have a rational design or is it ultimately meaningless?

[1] Educational philosophy derives also from the experiences of education. See Chapter 3 on "Contemporary Theories."

Is what we call mind a reality of its own or merely a form of matter in motion? Is the behavior of all organisms causally determined, or do some organisms, such as men, possess a measure of freedom?

With the rise of science many people believed metaphysics to be outmoded. Scientific findings seemed trustworthy because they could be measured, whereas metaphysical notions seemed to be unverifiable and to have no practical application. Today, however, we recognize that metaphysics and science are two different activities, each valuable in its own right. Both seek to make general statements, but metaphysics deals with concepts whose instances cannot be measured, such as "reality," "change," "self," and "spirit." This does not mean that metaphysicians disregard science. On the contrary, science itself often gives rise to problems about the nature of reality that metaphysicians seek to resolve.

Science also rests on metaphysical assumptions. Many people do not realize this fact. In his *Adventure of Ideas* Alfred North Whitehead writes. "No science can be more secure than the unconscious metaphysics which tacitly it presupposes." The nuclear physicist Max Planck agrees:

"The scientific world picture gained by experience . . . remains always a mere approximation, a more or less well divided model. As there is a material object behind every sensation, so there is a metaphysical reality behind everything that human experience shows to be real. . . ."[2]

Many of our greatest scientists, notably Albert Einstein, have felt compelled to formulate metaphysical conceptions *in consequence* of their scientific discoveries.

---

[2] Max Planck, "The Meaning and Limits of Exact Science," *Science* (1949), 319-327. Cf. Everett W. Hall, "Metaphysics," in Dagobert D. Runes, Ed., *Living Schools of Philosophy*, Littlefield, Adams, Ames, Iowa, 1956, p. 130: "Metaphysics affects action not by giving control over nature, not by offering physical devices which can be used for various purposes, but by shaping views as to what nature is and how it can and ought to be controlled, by indicating appropriate ends. It does so through a theory of ethics, based in a theory of values which, in turn, is based in a set of views concerning the nature of existence and of knowledge."

Certain philosophers, it is true, regard metaphysics as superfluous. They confine their attention to logic and the theory of knowledge. This position is defensible, but it is not widely held. Most philosophers maintain that theories of logic and knowledge inevitably are derived from metaphysical assumptions. There is, says Bertrand Russell, a "concealed metaphysic, usually unconscious in every writer on philosophy. Even if his subject is metaphysics, he is almost certain to have an uncritically believed system which underlies his explicit arguments"[3]

In recent years metaphysics has regained much of its former standing. Science no doubt has brought great material progress, but even if all man's material wants were satisfied, he would not be completely at home in the world. By nature man is a metaphysical being, possessed by a desire to draw from the diverse realms of public knowledge and private experience some understanding of the *ultimate* nature of things.

METAPHYSICS AND EDUCATION

In educational theory and practice metaphysics generates discussions of questions that lack scientific answers. For example, the metaphysical question whether human life has any purpose and, if so, what, is implicit in any study of biological evolution. If a student concludes from his study of evolution that the universe has no purpose, he may conclude that his life has meaning only as he personally puts meaning into it. In this case he must ask himself what goals in life he should pursue. Taking a metaphysical position will help him answer such questions.

Again, take the problem of the nature of mind. Teachers often say, "If Johnnie kept his mind on his work, he would have no trouble at all in school." But what does the teacher mean here by "mind"? Is the mind different from the body? How are the two related? Is the mind the actual source of thoughts? Perhaps what we call "mind" is not an entity at

[3] Bertrand Russell, "Dewey's New Logic," in Paul Schilpp, Ed., *The Philosophy of John Dewey*, Northwestern University Press, Evanston, Ill., 1939, p. 138.

all. Physiological and psychological studies of the brain have given us factual information and cyberneticians have compared the mind (or brain) to a computer. But such comparisons are crude; they do not satisfy our concern about the ultimate nature of the mind. Here again, knowing metaphysics and being able to think metaphysically helps the teacher when he is considering questions of ultimate meaning.

All teachers entertain notions about the nature of reality. They have views, however vague, about the nature of the universe, the destiny of man, the natural and the supernatural, permanence and change, and the ultimate purpose of things— matters that have concerned metaphysicians throughout the ages. Nothing, in fact, contributes more to continuous, patient, and careful reflection than the treatment of an educational problem in its metaphysical dimensions.

The number of metaphysical ideas is legion. For our purposes, however, they can be grouped according to certain "schools" of philosophic thought. The main schools, each with many subdivisions, are "idealism," "realism," and "pragmatism." If we consider what these schools have to say about the nature of reality and its relation to education, we shall be able to think more clearly about the question ourselves.

Before beginning our presentation, one word of caution: we are grouping philosophies into schools of thought for purposes of convenience, for ease of understanding. Philosophers also have to be studied separately and in their own right. Locke and Kant, for example, created systems that solved traditional philosophic problems afresh. Rousseau and Nietzsche were even more individualistic. And although both Kierkegaard and Sartre are existentialists, they differ in their views as much as they agree. After the student has studied philosophers in schools, he should go on to study them as individual thinkers.

IDEALIST METAPHYSICS AND EDUCATION

The philosophic idealist claims that ultimate reality is spiritual in nature rather than physical, mental rather than material.

When the ancient Eleatic philosopher Parmenides said, "What cannot be thought cannot be real," and when Schopenhauer proclaimed, "The world is my idea," they expressed the metaphysical outlook of idealism. The idealist does not deny the existence of the physical world around us—the world of houses, hills, stars, and cities with which our senses acquaint us. But he maintains that, real as these things are, they are not *ultimately* real. They are manifestations of a more fundamental incorporeal reality.

This reality may be either personal or impersonal. For the Christian idealist, ultimate reality is the God of three persons. It is not, as it is for Hegel, an impersonal Spirit. The Christian idealist agrees with other idealists in their conviction that man is a spiritual being who exercises free will and is personally responsible for his actions. Plato regards man's spirit as a "soul" emanating from an empyrean of perfect and external "ideas." Berkeley takes the orthodox Christian view that the soul is immortal, having been created by God to enjoy eternal life after probation on earth. According to Kant, man is both free and determined—free insofar as he is a spirit, determined to the extent that he is also a physical being subject to natural law. The Hegelian idealist regards man as a vital part of the Absolute—a spark, as it were, of an Eternal Spirit into which he is reabsorbed at death. Thus idealists agree that man is a spiritual being, but they disagree as to exactly how he is related to the ultimate spiritual reality from which he springs.

Idealists believe that the child is part of an ultimately spiritual universe and that he has a spiritual destiny to fulfill in accordance with his own potentialities. For this reason education must instill a closer intimacy between the child and the spiritual elements of nature; it must emphasize the innate harmony between man and the universe. When the child studies the natural world, he should not regard it as an enormous machine functioning soullessly and aimlessly. He should see the universe as possessing meaning and purpose.

The idealist teacher presides like Socrates over the birth of ideas, treated not as principles external to the student but as possibilities within him that need to be developed. The idealist teacher is also supposed to embody as fully as possible the finest characteristics of mankind and therefore to be worthy of emulation. With Socrates, Plato, and Kant he believes that knowledge is best "wrung out" of the student rather than "poured into" him. However, it is primarily *approved* subject matter that the teacher may "wring out," not usually the kind a student chooses for himself.

In view of prevailing skepticism about patriotism and love of country, we should note that many idealists uphold a philosophy of loyalty. Because in the long run the state is said to be a personality greater than any individual—a whole more important than any of its parts, the student should be taught to respect his country and the community into which he is born. He should study *sympathetically* the cultural foundations and ideals of his country and his community. His own freedom will grow only in proportion as he develops a sense of personal service to both community and nation.[4]

What, then, does education mean to the idealist? I know of no better definition than that of Herman H. Horne (1874-1946): "Education is the eternal process of superior adjustment of the physically and mentally developed, free, conscious, human being to God, as manifested in the intellectual, emotional, and volitional environment of man."[5]

REALIST METAPHYSICS AND EDUCATION

The basic principle of philosophic realism is that matter is the ultimate reality. Hills, trees, cities, and stars are not simply ideas in the minds of observing individuals, or even in the mind of an Eternal Observer. They exist in and of themselves, independently of the mind. Although realists agree about the

---

[4] Josiah Royce, *The Philosophy of Loyalty*, Macmillan, New York, 1908. Students interested in this particular phase of idealism would do well to study Royce's philosophy of loyalty. Royce insists that our allegiances should be not only local and national but also international.

[5] Herman H. Horne, *The Philosophy of Education*, Macmillan, New York, 1927, p. 285. Beginning p. 257 Horne analyzes the meaning of nearly every word in his definition. Especially valuable is his analysis of "freedom."

reality of matter, they disagree in some other respects and so may be divided into various subschools. Today the major groupings are "rational realism" on the one hand and "natural" or "scientific realism" on the other.

Rational Realism. This tradition may be divided into "classical realism" and "religious realism." The main form of religious realism is "scholasticism," the official philosophy of the Roman Catholic Church. Both schools bear the imprint of the Athenian philosopher Aristotle. But whereas classical realists look directly to Aristotle, the scholastics do so only indirectly, basing their philosophy on that of St. Thomas Aquinas. By harnessing the doctrines of Aristotle to the theology of the Church, Aquinas created a new Christian philosophy, later called "Thomism," in contrast to the modified Platonism espoused by most theologians of his time.

Classical and religious realists agree that the material world is real and exists outside the minds of those who observe it. Thomists, however, maintain that both matter and spirit have been created by God, Who constructed an orderly and rational universe out of His supreme wisdom and goodness. The fact that God created the universe is proof enough of its reality, for, say Thomists, anything divinely created must be real. Although not exactly more real than matter, spirit nevertheless is more important; it is a "higher" mode of being, because God himself is Spirit and He is perfect in every way. How do Thomists know all this? By revelation—from Biblical history, prophecy, and the teachings of Jesus Christ, which they affirm to be God's word for all mankind. But their knowledge, they state, is also attained by means other than faith; they get it from reason and experience, which are used not to contradict their faith but to support it. Thomists also declare that man is a fusion of the material and the spiritual, with body and soul forming one nature. We are free, they say, and responsible for our actions; but we are also immortal, having been placed on earth to love and honor our Creator and so earn immortal happiness.

Natural and Scientific Realism. This branch of philosophic realism accompanied the rise of science in Europe during the fifteenth and sixteenth centuries. Its leading spokesmen have been Francis Bacon, John Locke, David Hume, and John Stuart Mill. In this century they include Ralph Barton Perry, Alfred North Whitehead, and Bertrand Russell.

Skeptical and experimental in temper, natural realism maintains that philosophy should seek to imitate the rigor and objectivity of science. Since the world around us is real, it is the task of science rather than philosophy to investigate its properties; philosophy's function is to coordinate the concepts and findings of the different sciences. The most significant feature of the universe is that it is permanent and enduring. Change is real, but it takes place in accordance with permanent laws of nature, which give the universe a continuing structure. The world's permanence is the background against which changes occur and may be assessed. Natural realists either deny the existence of a spiritual realm or else maintain that its existence cannot be proved, so that it is of no importance philosophically.

Natural realists declare that man is a biological organism with a highly developed nervous system and an inherently social disposition. There is no need to suppose that his cultural achievements are due to a separate entity known as mind or soul. What we call "thought" is really a highly complex function of the organism that relates it to its environment—similar in kind, though not in degree, to such other functions as respiration, assimilation, and metabolism. Most scientific realists deny the existence of free will; they argue that the individual is determined by the impact of the physical and social environment on his genetic structure. What seems to be freedom of choice is really causal determination.

Since in the realist view the world exists independently of man and is governed by laws over which we have little control, the school should transmit a central core of subject matter that will acquaint the pupil with the world around him. The Catholic realist adds that since the order and harmony of the universe are the result of Divine creation, we should study nature as God's handiwork. In his view the prime purpose of education is to prepare the individual person for life in the hereafter. For the classical realist the purpose of education is to enable the pupil to become an *intellectually* well-balanced person, as against one who is simply "well adjusted" to his physical and social environment. Individual spontaneity and creativity are prized, as they are in other philosophies, but the products of these elusive attributes are subject to greater scrutiny.

PRAGMATIST METAPHYSICS AND EDUCATION

Although philosophic pragmatism is often regarded as an indigenous American philosophy, it is actually an outgrowth of the British empiricist tradition, which maintains that we can know only what our senses experience. In its theory of perpetual change, pragmatism looks back to Heraclitus, who lived before Socrates. The leading American pragmatists are Charles Sanders Peirce, William James, and John Dewey, all of whom differ in their methods and conclusions. Pierce's pragmatism is influenced by physics and mathematics, Dewey's by social science and biology. James's philosophy is personal, psychological, even religious. To a greater extent than realism or idealism, pragmatism has been influenced by conditions of the twentieth century. During the 1920s, for instance, it advocated individualism, while during the Depression it called for a greater social consciousness.

Pragmatism has been known by a variety of names, from "pragmaticism" (coined by Peirce) to "instrumentalism," "functionalism," and "experimentalism." In his later years, Dewey preferred "experimentalism" to "instrumentalism," partly because the latter sounded too materialistic. The principal themes of pragmatism are (1) the reality of change, (2) the essentially social and biological nature of man, (3) the relativity of values, and (4) the use of critical intelligence.

Pragmatists maintain that the world is neither dependent on nor independent of man's idea of it. Reality amounts to the "interaction" of the human being with his environment; it is the sum total of what we "experience." Man and his environment are "coordinate;" they are equally responsible for what is real.

The world has meaning only to the extent that man reads meaning into it. If the universe itself possesses some deeper purpose, it is hidden from man; and what man cannot experience cannot be real for him. Humanist in temper, pragmatism subscribes to the maxim that "man is the measure of all things." William James emphasizes the right of the educated individual to create his own reality, whereas Peirce and Dewey declare that the facts of reality are best established by experts, especially scientists.

The pragmatist believes that change is the essence of reality and that we must always be prepared to alter the way we do things. The ends and means of education must be flexible and open to continual revision. They must be pursued rationally and scientifically. Means are indigenous to their ends, and ends may derive from their means. Thus education itself is both an end and a means—an end in that it aims to improve man, and a means in that it is a way of doing so. Within education, discipline generally should not be opposed to the student's felt interests but should grow out of them.

The pragmatist maintains that since reality is created by a person's interaction with his environment, the child must study the world as it affects him. Just as the child cannot be considered apart from the environment in which he lives, so the school cannot be separated from life itself. Education *is* life and not a preparation for it. Formal subject matter should be linked wherever possible to the immediate problems that the child faces and that society is concerned to solve.

Unlike the realist and the idealist the pragmatist believes that human nature is fundamentally plastic and changeable. The pragmatist regards the child as an active organism, continually engaged in reconstructing and interpreting his own experiences. Because the child grows only by associating with others, he must learn to live in a community of individuals, to cooperate with them, and to adapt himself intelligently to social needs and aspirations.

The world view of pragmatism has certainly proved more

congenial to American students than the philosophies of realism or idealism. Also pragmatist philosophy has animated most programs in teacher education. It is not hard to see why this should be so. American culture is pluralist and heterogenous. America has no national religion, no ancient monarchy, and little veneration of the past. A dynamic and skeptical society appreciates a philosophy of change rather than of permanence; a calling into question of all things; and a theory that man by nature is enterprising and exploratory. When William James said that pragmatism implied an open-ended universe—a universe "with the lid off"—his American audience was delighted, for this was the world that many of them believed they lived in. Just as the American frontier could be pushed west to the limitless Pacific, so the world seemed full of infinite possibilities. Ingenious, optimistic, experimental, this was the pragmatist temper, and it was the temper of the American people.

CONCLUSION

From this brief overview we can see that although philosophy as a whole does not provide us with final answers to the questions it asks, it does offer a range of different possible answers that enlarge our thoughts and assist us in making personal choices. As I shall show in the next chapter, learning means more than accumulating facts that have been scientifically established; it also means speculating and advancing beyond the limits of such findings.

What, then, is the kind of knowledge that philosophy aims to impart? It is the kind that, as Bertrand Russell so well says, results from a "critical examination of the grounds of our convictions, prejudices, and beliefs." Questions that can be answered definitively belong mostly to science; other questions, speculative, prescriptive, and analytic, belong to philosophy. A study of the philosophy of education alerts us to the importance of these questions for the theory and practice of education. It enables us to examine philosophic questions for the light they throw on educational problems.

References

The entire issue of the *Harvard Educational Review*, XXVI, 2 (Spring 1956), is devoted to the relationship between philosophy and education. It contains essays by philosophers of different schools. Two recent comprehensive anthologies are Thomas O. Buford, Ed., *Toward a Philosophy of Education* (Holt, Rinehart and Winston, 1969, 518 pp.), and Christopher J. Lucas, Ed., *What is Philosophy of Education?* (Macmillan, 1969, 313 pp.). Buford's text has a glossary and extensive biographical notes; Lucas' has an excellent introduction.

The best textbook treating metaphysical aspects of education is Samuel Shermis, *Philosophic Foundations of Education* (American Book Co., 1967, 292 pp.), chs. 1-4.

On the schools of philosophy I recommend the following monographs: J. Donald Butler, *Idealism in Education* (1966, 145 pp.); Ernest E. Bayles, *Pragmatism in Education* (1966, 145 pp.); and William Oliver Martin, *Realism in Education* (1969, 198 pp.), all published by Harper and Row. The classic text covering the entire field is John S. Brubacher, *Modern Philosophies of Education*, first published, 1939, now in its 4th edition (McGraw-Hill, 1969, 393 pp.).

Students majoring in educational philosophy will find a useful, well organized handbook in *Philosophy of Education: An Organization of Topics and Selected Sources* by Harry S. Broudy, Michael J. Parson, Ivan A. Snook, and Ronald D. Szoke (University of Illinois Press, Urbana, 1967, 287 pp.).

Students who desire to learn more about philosophy itself, and to have fun doing so, will enjoy C. E. M. Joad's *Philosophy* (Fawcett World Library, New York, 1962). Students with an interest in metaphysics will find much to challenge them in W. E. Kennick and M. Lazerowitz, *Metaphysics: Readings and Appraisals* (Prentice-Hall, 1966, 387 pp.).

2

Knowledge and Value

In the previous chapter I argued that the theory and practice of education presuppose ideas about human nature and the nature of reality that are ultimately of a philosophical character. I pointed out that if the teacher is to do his life's work wisely and well, he must confront and debate and perhaps change the metaphysical assumptions by which his conduct is partly guided. To help the teacher do this, I considered some important metaphysical theses that have in fact influenced education. But education presupposes more than metaphysics; it also presupposes ideas about the nature of knowledge and the nature of what is valuable. To understand these ideas in their clearest and most general terms, we turn to philosophy.

Knowledge is the principal stock in trade of educators. A teacher is preoccupied chiefly with the intellectual development of his students. Even when he is concerned with their physical health and emotional well-being, he must base his judgments on reliable knowledge. It is therefore important for the teacher to think out for himself philosophically what knowledge ultimately amounts to.

The branch of philosophy that deals with knowledge is called "epistemology." The philosopher as epistemologist reflects on the nature of knowledge as such. What is there, he asks, that is common to all the different activities that are involved in knowing? What is the difference between knowing and, say, believing? What can we know beyond the information provided by the senses? What is the relation of the act of knowing to the thing that is known? How can we show that knowledge is "true"?

Unlike the scientist, the epistemologist is interested in concepts rather than facts. The task of the psychologist, for example, is to find out how people actually think and feel. The task of the epistemologist, on the other hand, is to consider what is meant by such psychological concepts as "feeling," "perception," "learning," and "reinforcement," and to judge whether the psychologist is applying them correctly. If the psychologist is not doing so, he is misdescribing the facts.

From the point of view of the teacher, one of the most important distinctions made in epistemology is that between the different types of knowledge. We will consider what these types of knowledge are and then look more generally at the epistemologies proposed by the leading schools of philosophy.

Types of Knowledge

Revealed Knowledge. Simply put, revealed knowledge may be described as knowledge that God has disclosed to man. In His omniscience God inspired certain men to write down truths that He revealed to them, so that these truths might be known thereafter by all mankind. For Christians and Jews the word of God is contained in the Bible, for Muslims in the Koran, for Hindus in the Bhagavad-Gita and the Upanishads. Because it is the word of God, it is true forever. If it were not, God would be either ignorant or deceitful, which is to say that He would not be God. But although the truths recorded are supernatural, the language in which they are written is not. Hence religious scholars spend much time arguing over the precise meaning of words and expressions in the sacred texts. These arguments are not exercises in hairsplitting. For the religious believer the most important truths in the world lie in the words over which theologians argue. The essence of textual interpretation is to bring to light the eternal truths that are locked in these words.

Intuitive Knowledge. Revealed knowledge is God-given and external to man. Intuitive knowledge is knowledge that a person finds within himself in a moment of insight. Insight or intuition is the sudden eruption into consciousness of an idea or conclusion produced by a long process of unconscious work. All of a sudden we see the solution to a problem with which our unconscious has been at grips for days, months, or even years. It is this prior labor of the unconscious that gives the moment of insight its exhilaration and its seeming certainty. We feel sure of our insights just because, without being aware of it, we have worked so hard for them. We are exhilarated by them because the psychic energy, so long invested in the search for a solution, is released suddenly in the sheer pleasure of discovery. We are exhilarated, too, because this very discharge of energy gives us a sense of the fullness of our mental powers.

We must distinguish, however, between the act of intuition and intuitive knowledge proper. Some formative insight or illumination seems necessary to all great intellectual achievements. Philosophic theses, scientific theories, and works of art all seem to be generated out of some primary intuition, which is then elaborated and refined. But whatever its origins, a completed scientific theory is not a form of intuitive knowledge. It is logically consistent and is testable by observation or experimentation or both. When a scientific theory is proposed as a claim to knowledge, it is submitted not as a personal insight of its creator but as a publicly verifiable hypothesis.

What, then, is intuitive knowledge? It is knowledge that is

proposed, and accepted, on the strength of the imaginative vision or private experience of the person proposing it. The truths embodied in works of art are a form of intuitive knowledge. All great writers—Homer, Shakespeare, Proust—tell us truths about the heart of man. We would not dream of testing these truths by observations or calculations or experiments, because these truths are not hypotheses. They are offered as insights, and we ourselves recognize them as true intuitively. Mystical writings, autobiographies, and essays of all kinds are reflections of intuitive knowledge.

We ourselves also possess a good deal of intuitive knowledge of our own, especially about people. It is knowledge that we have picked up from our experience of others and our experience of ourselves. We have reflected on it, certainly, but we have not submitted it to any systematic rational scrutiny or observational testing. We have not done so because we do not need to. It is a knowledge or awareness that we deepen, broaden, and correct in the course of our experience.

Rational Knowledge. This is knowledge that we obtain by the exercise of reason alone unaccompanied by observation of actual states of affairs. The principles of formal logic and pure mathematics are paradigms of rational knowledge. Their truth is demonstrable by abstract reasoning alone. Take the logical principle that two contradictory statements cannot both be true at once, that the statements "Fido is a dog" and "Fido is not a dog" cannot both be predicated of the same object at the same time. Or take the principle that if A is greater than B and B is greater than C, then A is greater than C; for example, if a Boeing 747 is bigger than a Flying Fortress, and a Flying Fortress is bigger than a Piper Cub, then a 747 is bigger than a Piper Cub. Both these principles can be illustrated by actual instances, but both are true independently of such instances. The principles of rational knowledge may be applied *to* sense experience, but they are not deduced *from* it. Unlike the truths of intuitive knowledge, they are valid regardless of our feelings about them and they are valid universally.

Rational knowledge is not without its limitations. It is fundamentally abstract and formal. It deals with logical relations and impersonal meanings and disregards emotional needs and actual states of affairs. Because we live emotionally among states of affairs, rational knowledge alone is hardly sufficient. We also need intuitive and empirical knowledge, and often we need them more. It is also open to debate how much rational knowledge actually is valid universally and how much merely seems so. All of us are to some extent culture-bound, and it may be that even the principles of formal logic are valid only for persons who use European languages and think in the mental categories that these languages embody. It has also been questioned whether rational knowledge ultimately rests on rational demonstration. According to one school of thought, for example, the principles of pure mathematics are grounded in a basic *intuition* of successiveness.

Empirical Knowledge. Especially important nowadays is empirical knowledge or knowledge that is confirmed by the evidence of the senses. By seeing, hearing, smelling, feeling, and tasting, we form our conception of the world around us. Knowledge, therefore, is composed of ideas formed in accordance with observed—or sensed—facts. Whereas the rationalist tells us to "think things through," the empiricist advises us to "look and see."

The paradigm of empirical knowledge is modern science. Scientific hypotheses are tested by observation or by experiments to find which hypothesis accounts most satisfactorily for a certain set of phenomena. Nevertheless, a hypothesis is never proved or disproved absolutely. It is only shown to be more or less "probable." Empirical probability may come close at times to certainty but can never actually attain it. The reason for this is that we can never be certain that the future will resemble the past, and hence we can never be absolutely sure that phenomena that have behaved in certain ways hitherto will behave in exactly those ways hereafter.

It should also be pointed out that our senses may at times deceive us, as when a stick that is really straight looks bent in water. As Socrates asked just before he drank the hemlock, "Have our senses truth in them? Are they not . . . inaccurate witnesses?" Moreover, our senses are conditioned by our preconceptions. We tend to perceive what it is within our power to conceive. Thus we perceive space as a permanent background within which unique events occur sequentially in time. This apprehension of space and time is almost certainly a phenomenon of our culture at a certain stage of its development.

Authoritative Knowledge. We accept a good deal of knowledge as true not because we have checked it out ourselves but because it is vouched for by authorities in the field. I accept without question that Canberra is the capital of Australia, that light travels at 186,281 miles per second, and that the Battle of Waterloo took place in 1815. I feel no need to verify these facts, any more than I feel the need to work out for myself the table of logarithms. I take them for granted because I find them in encyclopedias and other works written by experts. I take the experts in turn at their word because I wish to preserve my psychic energy for personal projects that utilize or go beyond established facts. The world is too large a place for me to verify personally all that occurs in it.

What knowledge I take for granted depends on my needs and interests. If I want to know, as items of information, what Cubism is or what Newton's laws of motion are, I look up Cubism and Newton in an encyclopedia. But if information is all I am looking for, information is all I get. If I wish to *understand* Cubism or Newtonian mechanics, I must work out the principles of these things for myself. Needless to say, I do not reinvent Cubism or mechanics, but I think through the principles on which they are based until I see the "point" of them. I understand Cubism when I see the artistic objectives that the Cubists set themselves and the means they used to attain them. I understand Newton's laws of motion when I see the reasoning on which they are based, the conclusions to which they lead, and the evidence massed in their favor.

What I take for granted, however, is already knowledge. Newton's laws of motion have been confirmed scientifically; they are empirical knowledge. Thus the term "authoritative knowledge" is more psychological than epistemological in import. It denotes not the nature of those things that I know but the manner of my knowing them. It refers not to those cultural products we call knowledge as such but to the way in which I appropriate these products. "Authoritative knowledge" is established knowledge that I accept on someone's authority.

So far we have considered some of the different categories of what passes for knowledge. Let us now take a broader view and inquire what the leading schools of philosophy have said about knowledge in general and its relation to education.

Idealist Epistemology and Education

Within the idealist tradition different philosophers have produced different theories of knowledge. Plato, in agreement with Socrates, maintained that knowledge acquired through the senses must always remain uncertain and incomplete, since the material world is only a distorted copy of a more perfect sphere of being. True knowledge is the product of reason alone, for reason is the faculty that discerns the pure spiritual forms of things beyond their material embodiments.

Hegel elaborated the platonic concept that knowledge is valid only insofar as it forms a system. Since ultimate reality is rational and systematic, our knowledge of reality is true to the extent that it, too, is systematic. The more comprehensive the system of our knowledge and the more consistent the ideas it embraces, the more truth it may be said to possess. This principle usually is referred to as the "coherence theory" of truth. It is based on the view that a particular item of knowledge becomes significant to the extent that it is seen in its total context. Hence all ideas and theories must be validated according to their "coherence" within a continuously developing system of knowledge.

Following Kant, most modern idealists maintain that the essence of knowing is the imposition of meaning and order on information gathered by the senses. The purpose of teaching is not so much to present the student with a mass of information as to help him to impose order and meaning on it. Some idealists, known as "personalists," also maintain that the student should relate this information to his own previous experiences so that what he learns is significant to him personally.

Realist Epistemology and Education

The realist rejects the Kantian view that the mind imposes its own categories, such as "substantiality" and "causality," on the data of the senses. On the contrary, says the realist, the world we perceive is not a world that we have recreated mentally but the world as it is. Substantiality, causality, and the order of nature are not a projection of the mind but are features of things themselves. Admittedly, natural science yields a different picture of the world than everyday experience. The sturdy table on which I write these words is, for the physicist, a collection of invisible particles. But from this it follows only that with different instruments different aspects of the world are observed, not that these aspects are appearances synthesized by the observer himself.

For the realist, then, an idea or proposition is true when it "corresponds" with those features of the world that it purports to describe. A hypothesis about the world is not true simply because it "coheres" with knowledge. If new knowledge coheres with old, it is because the old is true, that is, it is because the old knowledge *corresponds* to what is the case. Coherence then does not create truth. It is rather that, when two or more theories about related features of the world correspond to the features they describe, they will naturally support one another.

True knowledge, then, is knowledge that corresponds to the world as it is. In the course of time the human race has put together a stock of knowledge whose truth has repeatedly been confirmed. To impart a selection of this knowledge to the growing person is the school's most important task. The initiative in education, therefore, lies with the teacher as transmitter of the cultural heritage. It is the teacher, not the student, who must decide what subject matter should be studied in class. If this subject matter can be made to satisfy the student's personal needs and interests, so much the better. But satisfying the student personally is far less important than imparting the right subject matter. To instruct the student in the knowledge that matters most is the true end of education; satisfying the student is only a means to this end, a useful teaching strategy.

Pragmatist Epistemology and Education

Pragmatists believe the mind to be active and exploratory rather than passive and receptive. The mind does not confront a world that is separate and apart from it. Rather, the known world is formed in part by the mind that knows it. Truth does not lie solely in the correspondence of human ideas to an external reality, because reality for man depends in part on the ideas by which he explains it. Knowledge is produced by a "transaction" between man and his environment, and truth is a property of knowledge. What then does truth amount to?

Pragmatists have been charged with claiming that an idea is true if it "works." The charge applies, if at all, only to William James, who maintained that an idea is true if it has favorable consequences for the person who holds it. Other pragmatists, such as Peirce and Dewey, insist that an idea is true only if it has satisfactory consequences *when objectively and if possible scientifically tested.* For the typical pragmatist, then, the truth of an idea depends on the consequences that are observed objectively when the idea is put into operation.

Pragmatists also maintain that the "method of intelligence" is the ideal way to acquire knowledge. We grasp things best, they say, by locating and solving problems. Faced with a problem, the intelligence proposes hypotheses to deal with it. The hypothesis that solves the problem most successfully is the hypothesis that explains the facts of the problem. It is what Dewey calls a "warranted assertion," a claim to knowledge that has been confirmed objectively and operationally and may serve as a basis for generating further hypotheses for further problems.

According to the pragmatist, the teacher should construct learning situations around particular problems whose solution will lead his pupils to a better understanding of their social and physical environment. Instead of following the traditional structure of subject matter, both teacher and class should draw on whatever knowledge proves useful in solving the particular problem with which they are engaged, such as "transportation through the ages," "contemporary sexual mores," or "life in an

Indian village." The same procedure should be followed in learning the skills of reading, writing, and arithmetic. All subjects, says the pragmatist, become more meaningful to the student and so more easily mastered when the student can use them as means for satisfying needs and interests of his own.

According to the pragmatist, a young person is a natural learner because he is naturally curious. He will learn most from whatever he feels stimulated to explore and think about. The teacher should foster this spirit of inquiry. Instead of instructing the student in subject matter prescribed for him by others, the teacher should encourage the student (a) to learn what he feels curious about and (b) to feel a curiosity about subjects that matter, such as science, literature, and history. Precept (b) is important, because the teacher would be irresponsible if he encouraged the student to pursue his every whim and fancy. The point for the pragmatist is that the child should learn from curiosity, while the teacher should stimulate curiosity about subjects that will fully reward it.

VALUES AND EDUCATION

Values abound everywhere in education; they are involved in every aspect of school practice; they are basic to all matters of choice and decision-making. Using values, teachers evaluate students and students evaluate teachers. Society evaluates courses of study, school programs, and teaching competence; and society itself is evaluated by educators. When we pass judgment on educational practices, when we estimate the worth of an education policy, what kind of values do we employ?

The general study of values is known as "axiology." It concerns itself with three main questions: (1) whether values are subjective or objective, that is, personal or impersonal; (2) whether values are changing or constant; and (3) whether there are hierarchies of value. Let us examine these issues briefly.

1. To say that there are objective values is to claim that there are values that exist in their own right regardless of human preferences. Such values as goodness, truth, and beauty are cosmic realities; they are part of the nature of things. Certain things are objectively true. Certain actions and certain qualities are inherently good. Certain things are beautiful in themselves. Education has an objective value; it is worthwhile in itself.

To maintain that values are subjective is to claim that they reflect personal preferences. To be valuable is to be valued by someone. Whatever is valuable is so not in itself but because we happen to value it. To say that education is valuable, for example, is to say that one values education oneself or that some people value education. It is not to claim that education is worthwhile regardless of whether anyone thinks so.

2. Some people argue that there are values that are absolute and eternal. These values are as valid today as they were in the past, and they are valid for everyone regardless of race or class. Charity, it is sometimes argued, is a good for all men everywhere at all times. Other people maintain that all values are relative to men's desires. As our desires change, so do the values that express them. Desires, and so values, change in response to new historical conditions, new religions, new findings in science, new developments in technology, advances in education, and so forth. These values may be arrived at empirically and tested publicly; they may be the creation of the rational mind; or they may be the result of strong belief. We may ask, for example, whether grading is valuable. We cannot say absolutely yes or no. It may or may not be, depending on the persons involved, the purposes it serves, the way it is handled, and the results it produces. How would we know? Chiefly by applying standards or criteria that educated men accept. Paradoxically, however, such standards are closely linked to absolute values, or at least to values that are more or less permanent. For how can we know the extent to which our values change if we do not have something permanent against which to assess the change?

As a rule, young people prefer to keep their values personal and relative. In the way they prize things they want to remain flexible and openminded. Indeed, the very thought of having anything absolute disturbs them profoundly . . . except, perhaps, when it comes to absolutes they may desire, such as freedom, love, peace, justice, and human understanding.

3. Just what attitude the thoughtful person takes to values depends on his general philosophy. As I shall show, the philosophic idealist maintains that there is a fixed hierarchy of values in which spiritual values are higher than material ones. The idealist ranks religious values high because, he says, they help us realize our ultimate goal, unity with the spiritual order. The philosophic realist also believes in a hierarchy of values, but he ranks rational and empirical values high because they help us adjust to objective reality, the laws of nature, and the rules of logic. The philosophic pragmatist denies that there is a fixed hierarchy of values. For him one activity is likely to be as good as another if it satisfies an urgent need and possesses instrumental value. He is sensitive to the values that society prizes, but he believes that it is more important to test values empirically than to contemplate them rationally. He believes so because he thinks that all particular values are merely instruments for the attainment of better values.

It is desirable to study values scientifically as well as philosophically. If, for example, we can show that Americans prize the same values as do other people elsewhere, we shall have come a long way toward establishing foundations on which international understanding can be built. Elaborate classifications have been made of what men *in fact* value highly as contrasted with what they *say* they value. The results are startling and should be studied by every educator. The findings of the social scientist provide both educator and philosopher with facts for deep reflection.[1]

---

[1] For example, in 1969 Louis Harris & Associates surveyed a cross section of four thousand Americans on a wide range of attitudes and values. The poll revealed a continued preference for basic values, although the Puritan ethic of hard work and personal success did not rank as highly as might have been expected, coming below a desire for greater tranquility and more leisure time. Given a choice between making more money and getting more time off, only forty-five percent opted for the money. In short, we do not appear to be as compulsively dissatisfied and materialistic as we are often

ETHICS AND EDUCATION

Education is widely regarded as a moral enterprise. Teachers are always drawing attention to what ought to be said and done and how students ought to behave. They are concerned with imparting moral values and improving individual and social behavior.

What kind of moral behavior should a teacher advocate in his classes? Should he seek to promote the behavior that he values or the behavior valued by his community? Should he encourage the growth of certain character traits that he believes are desirable or should he let the child's character form itself in response to the expectation of the classroom peer group? One's answers to these questions will depend on one's ethical attitudes. Any teacher who takes his vocation seriously must seek to answer the questions and justify his attitudes. He will be assisted in doing so by a formal study of ethics.

Ethics is the study of values in the realm of human conduct. It deals with such questions as: What is the good life for all men? How ought we to behave? It is concerned with providing "right" values as the basis for "right" actions. At one time ethical systems were linked to religions. Today, however, the ethical systems of the Western world, although largely derived from religious teachings, are usually justified on other grounds. The United States has separated church and state and as a result religious teaching has been banned in American public schools. But this ban in turn has stimulated a desire to substitute some kind of moral training.

---

accused of being. Sixty percent of teen-agers and seventy-five percent of adults opposed pre-marital sex. Seventy-five percent of people considered the use of marijuana to be a "very serious" problem. There were, however, big differences between adults and young people and between whites and blacks, which suggests that many of the nation's values will change "dramatically" in the next decade, when present teen-agers become adults, when the number of blacks increases (from eleven percent of the population to an estimated seventeen percent), and when the college-educated will form forty-five percent of the population instead of the present thirty percent.

Two types of ethical theory are important here: "intuitionism" and "naturalism." Intuitionists assert that moral values are apprehended by the individual directly. We grasp the rightness or wrongness of something by means of an inborn moral sense. The moral values we apprehend in this way are right in themselves. Their rightness cannot be proved logically or tested empirically; it can only be intuited.

Naturalists maintain that moral values should be determined by careful studies of the ascertainable consequences to which they give rise. For example, if one believes that premarital sexual relations are morally wrong, one should do so not because of ethical judgments already made on the subject but as a consequence of personal observation or scientific studies of the effects of such relations. A person who accepts the naturalistic interpretation of ethics chooses or justifies moral values according to what scientific investigations reveal about right and wrong behavior and what *examined* life experiences suggest is the best way for human beings to conduct themselves. In brief, the naturalist maintains that moral values should be founded on an objective examination of the practical consequences of any act of human conduct.

Can moral values be taught in the same sense that factual knowledge is taught? Socrates sought to answer this question. Assuming that moral virtues were latent in each individual, he maintained that the teacher could bring these values into the student's consciousness. Virtue, we may say, can be taught, if by teaching virtue we mean helping students become aware of it. But will the student act on what he has learned? We all recognize that a student can hardly be said to have really learned something unless he is able to act on it.[2] Here then is the rub. If by teaching and learning we mean simply imparting and acquiring knowledge of what morals are, then values are teachable. Teachers can also test students to find out how much they know about moral values and can assist them in choosing

---

[2] Socrates also thought that, assuming that the teacher himself were virtuous, then the more virtue were taught to the student, the more virtue the student would practice. I would reply: The more the virtuous teacher presides over the *practice* of virtue, the more virtue the student will practice.

between alternative courses of action. But no teacher can guarantee, even after performing his task assiduously, doing all he can to get a student to know what ethical values are, and helping him to choose certain values for his own life, that a student will not cheat on a test. The most a teacher can expect is that the student (a) *knows* what is right and what is wrong, (b) knows *why* it is so, and (c) has some idea of what he *ought* to do about what he knows. If, in addition, the student actually engages in right conduct, the teacher will have been more than amply rewarded for his efforts.[3]

AESTHETICS AND EDUCATION

Aesthetics is the study of values in the realm of beauty. Aesthetic values usually are difficult to assess because they are likely to be personal and subjective. A particular work of art evokes varying responses from different people. *De gustibus non disputandum est.* Who is to say which response is the more appropriate?

Who, indeed, unless we believe that there are objective aesthetic values, in which case we may choose to rely on the decision of experts as to what is good art. We may judge beauty by using criteria said to be authoritative, and may claim that any work of art that scores low on these criteria will have a hard time finding its place in history. Objective criteria are useful to the novice, and they serve as enduring standards of criticism. Textbooks in literature, art, and music rely on these standards when informing students on matters involving assessment and appreciation. The fact, however, that authoritative critics may differ widely when assessing a work of art brings us back to our previous question: Who is to say which response is truly appropriate? Unfortunately we cannot look to science for answers to this question. Scientific knowledge is largely irrelevant to the judgment of a work of art.

[3] I discuss these ideas in my treatment of the concept of teaching in the chapter on analysis.

Through the centuries an important question discussed in aesthetics has been this: Should art be representative, or should it be the product of the creator's imagination? According to the first view, art should faithfully reflect life and human experience. We should clearly recognize the autumnal scene or fading sunset depicted in a landscape painting. We should be delighted by a still life of a bowl of flowers, each flower etched so well, its petals so lifelike, that we feel impelled to reach out and touch them! According to the second view, the artist expresses himself spontaneously about any aspect of life that interests him. "A picture," said Degas, "must never be a copy. . . . The air we see in the paintings of the old masters is never the air we breathe." The artist is on his own. He creates out of his personal drives and experiences. He expresses his feelings about the beauty or ugliness of the world and, perhaps, shows what he thinks the world should be. In this view, the creator enjoys limitless freedom to use his medium in a way that fulfills the creative urge within him.

In both views, questions arise as to the proper subject matter and scope of art. Some people maintain that if art is an expression of life, it should deal with *all* of life: the ugly, the aberrant, the grotesque, and the unique. Others believe that art should perform a social function. The artist should speak to all the men of his time, not to a tiny clique now or hereafter. Still others are skeptical of the so-called social responsibility of the artist. Society changes. An artist born in one generation may be creating for the next. Shall he be condemned for failing to please his contemporaries? An artist who has pleased his critics is probably at the end of his inventive powers, for critics tend to judge in accordance with accepted standards. Indeed, the artist rejected by the critics may well be the true innovator.

Idealist Values and Education

For the idealist, values and ethics are absolute. The good, the true, and the beautiful do not change fundamentally from generation to generation, or from society to society. In their essence they remain constant. They are not man-made but are part of the very nature of the universe.

The student, says the idealist, should be taught enduring values and how to live by them, for they put him in harmony with the greater spiritual whole to which he belongs. He should realize that evil offends not merely himself, or society, or even mankind as a whole, but the very soul of the universe. His values become significant only to the extent that they relate to the ultimately spiritual order of the universe, an order that the teacher can illuminate for the student.

Evil, says the idealist, is incomplete good rather than a positive thing in itself. It results from the disorganization and lack of system still present in the universe. As the Spirit present in the universe expresses itself more and more fully, the world will become more rational and less imperfect, and evil will gradually disappear. In any school system there are, for the idealist teacher, no really bad children, but only those who have strayed away from, or do not fully comprehend, the fundamental moral order of the universe.[4]

Plato maintained that the good life is possible only within a good society. In *The Republic*, he describes an ideal society ruled by a highly virtuous elite of philosopher-kings. Hegel declared that the individual derives his understanding and practice of virtue from the virtuous state of which he is a part. Kant's ideal community consisted of men who treated one another as ends rather than means. His famous "categorical imperative" states that we should always act as though our individual actions were to become a universal law of nature, binding on all men in similar circumstances.

[4] The same is true of ugliness, which, says the idealist, is beauty incomplete or disorganized. Cf. J. Donald Butler, *Four Philosophies and Their Practice in Education and Religion*, Harper, New York, 1957, pp. 534 ff. As a religious idealist, Butler asks, "Since the One who alone . . . has ultimate being, is good, how can evil have ultimate being?"

Assuming that no one would wish to see his own wrongdoing universalized, we should expect anyone following Kant's maxim always to refrain from doing evil. When a pupil misbehaves, the teacher would ask him what would happen if *everyone* behaved in this way. Is he setting a good example for his classmates to follow? (The teacher might also ask himself whether *he* is a good example for his students to follow!) Infractions of discipline are conceived as expressions of selfishness, to be punished in accordance with the moral principles that have been incorporated in the common culture over time. In the idealist view these principles are generally rooted in religion or at least in a view that life is eternal. In this respect here is a beautiful passage by Herman H. Horne, reflecting as well as any passage I know the prevailing mood of idealism:

"No man is ever all he can be . . . . His purposes are not ended with his life, nor does he live in a spent world . . . . Age does not wither, nor custom stale, the philosopher's love of truth, the artist's love of beauty, or the saint's love of virtue . . . . There is always more to know, and to love, and to do . . . . Man does not limit his will to know, to enjoy, to achieve, to his life's unknown term of years. His plans bridge the chasm of death; they call for unending time . . . ."[5]

Realist Values and Education

Realists agree with idealists that fundamental values are basically permanent, but they differ among themselves in their reasons for thinking so. Classical realists agree with Aristotle that there is a universal moral law, available to reason, that is binding on all of us as rational beings. Christian religious realists agree that we can understand much of this moral law by using reason, but they insist that the law has been established by God, Who has endowed us with the rational faculty to apprehend it. We may be able to understand the moral law

[5] Herman H. Horne, *The Philosophy of Education*, Macmillan, New York, 1927, p. 278.

without divine aid, but because our nature has been corrupted by Original Sin, we cannot practice it without the help of God. Scientific realists deny that values have any supernatural sanction. Good is that which accommodates us to our environment, evil that which estranges us. Because both human nature and physical nature are constant, the values that accommodate the one to the other are constant also. It is true that social institutions and practices vary considerably in various parts of the world, but basic values remain the same. Whereas idealists hold man to be perfectible, scientific realists accept him as he is, imperfect.

Realists agree that teachers should impart certain well-defined values. The basic moral and aesthetic standards that we teach the child should not be affected by temporary issues. The child should understand clearly the nature of right and wrong, respecting what is objectively good and beautiful regardless of changes in moral and aesthetic fashion.

Classical realists insist that despite concentration on subject matter, schools should produce individuals who are well-rounded, in the Aristotelian sense of being moderate and temperate in all things. The child should be taught to live by absolute and universal moral standards, because what is right is right for man in general and not simply for the members of a particular race or society. It is important for children to acquire good habits, for virtue does not come automatically to man but has to be learned.

Christian religious realists declare that naturalistic ethics are inadequate, for man has been created to transcend the natural and attain the supernatural. The true purpose of moral education is the salvation of souls. The child should be taught to keep his soul in a state of grace, that is, filled with Divine Grace and free from mortal sin. He should seek good and avoid evil, not only because reason so prescribes but also because it is God's will that he should.

The Christian religious realist trains man's will as well as his intellect. Although God offers salvation, the individual must decide whether to accept or reject it. The will should therefore be "habituated" to making the right choices. Because human nature has been corrupted by Original Sin, education has an essentially corrective role to play. Firm discipline is needed to eliminate bad habits and cultivate good ones. But reason is not sovereign. Indeed, a complete understanding of the nature of things lies beyond the power of reason, and we must depend on faith to carry us through. Reason should support faith, for God has given it to us so that we may come to know Him better.

The scientific realist teaches that right and wrong come from our understanding of nature and not from religious principles. Morality should be based on what scientific investigation has shown to be beneficial to man as the highest species of animal. Disease is evil and health is good. We must promote the good by taking measures to improve our genetic constitution and overcome evil by improving the environment in which we live.[6]

I close this sketch of realist values by asking, with realist Harry S. Broudy, "How can life be both subjectively and objectively good?" The answer, he says, is "self-cultivation"—cultivation of the individual's capacity to achieve enduring values in both intellectual and moral realms of experience:

"For education, this has always meant the appropriation by the individual of the best and noblest of the cultural resources of his time. It has meant becoming a connoisseur in every area of human life, so that the individual not only lives but lives well . . . . [But] there is a sense in which problems and answers are neither old nor new; it is the sense in which they are timeless structures revealed in a timeless insight into the form of universal truths."[7]

---

[6] Many scientific realists are also religiously minded. If so, they treat religion and science as two different aspects of truth. Not necessarily in conflict with one another, religion and science lead to a greater understanding of the ultimate mystery of the universe: "The heavens declare the glory of God and the firmament showeth His handiwork."

[7] Harry S. Broudy, "New Problems and Old Solutions," The Kansas State College, Emporia, Studies in Contemporary Educational Thought, **XL**, 11 (November 1960), 20-24.

Pragmatist Values and Education

For the pragmatist, values are relative. Ethical and moral canons are not permanent but must alter as cultures and societies change. This is not to claim that moral values should fluctuate from month to month. It is to say that no particular precept should be regarded as universally binding irrespective of the circumstances in which it is exercised. "Thou shalt not kill" is not an absolute principle; on occasion it may be right to kill, in order to defend oneself, for example, or to save the life of another. The child should learn how to make difficult moral decisions not by recourse to rigidly prescribed principles but by deciding which course of action is likely to produce the best results for the greatest number of human beings.

Pragmatists urge us to test the worth of our values in the same way that we test the truth of our ideas. We should consider the problems of human affairs impartially and scientifically and choose the values that seem most likely to resolve them. These values should not be imposed on us by a higher authority. They should be agreed on after open, informed discussion based on objective evidence.

The more complex a society becomes, the greater the demands it makes on the individual. But the pragmatist rejects any concept of individualism that leads to social exploitation and also any social arrangement that submerges the individuality of the person. Dewey calls the blending of individual thought and group sanction a "critical engagement." The utopian community he envisions is built by people who have the courage to think independently and yet relate themselves to the group.

"My belief in the Absolute," wrote William James, "must run the gauntlet of my other beliefs." It "clashes with other truths of mine whose benefits I hate to give up on its account." Such is the moral attitude of the pragmatist, whose doctrine, says James, "unstiffens our theories," and, if anything, "widens the search for God." What, then, is the moral ground of the pragmatist? Let William James describe his doctrine in his own inimitable way:

"She [pragmatism] has in fact no prejudices whatever, no obstructive dogmas, no rigid canons of what shall count as proof. She is completely genial. She will entertain any hypothesis, she will consider any evidence . . . . Her only test of probable truth is what works best . . . what fits every part of life best, and what combines with the collectivity of experience's demands, nothing being omitted . . . . You see how democratic she is. Her manners are as various and flexible, her resources as rich and endless, and her conclusions as friendly as those of mother nature."[8]

These last two chapters have given us some idea of philosophy's contribution to education. This contribution will be spelled out in greater detail in the next chapter on theories of education, where the views of educators themselves are examined. Although these theories are related to the philosophic themes we have discussed, they deal with issues specific to the actual practice of education.

References

On general epistemology I recommend three works: Roderick Chisholm, *Theory of Knowledge* (Prentice-Hall, 1966, 117 pp.); Michael Polanyi, *Personal Knowledge* (University of Chicago Press, 1958, 428 pp.); and John V. Canfield and Franklin H. Donnell, Ed., *Readings in the Theory of Knowledge* (Appleton-Century-Crofts, 1964, 520 pp.).

There are few comprehensive treatments of the significance for education of philosophic theories of knowledge. The most helpful discussion of the subject is probably Philip G. Smith, *Philosophy of Education: An Introduction* (Harper and Row, 1965, 276 pp.), ch. 4. (Ch. 7 on values is also good.) A useful book of readings is Donald Vandenburg, Ed., *Theory of Knowledge and Problems of Education* (University of Illinois Press, 1969, 302 pp.). On

[8] William James, *Pragmatism*, Longmans, Green, New York, 1907, pp. 80-81.

criteria for "true" knowledge from the analytic point of view, see Israel Scheffler, *Conditions of Knowledge: An Introduction to Epistemology and Education* (Scott, Foresman, 1965, 117 pp.).

On values and ethics, see William K. Frankena, *Ethics* (Prentice-Hall, 1963, 109 pp.) and A. Oldenquist, Ed., *Readings in Moral Philosophy* (Houghton, Mifflin, 1965, 364 pp.). My favorite is Jacob Bronowski's well-written *Science and Human Values* (Harper, 1965, 119 pp.).

On values in relation to education, see R. S. Peters, *Ethics and Education* (Scott, Foresman, 1967, 235 pp.); John Wilson et al., *Introduction to Moral Education* (Penguin, 1967, 463 pp.); John Martin Rich, *Education and Human Values* (Addison-Wesley, 1968, 163 pp.); and three anthologies: Theodore Brameld and Stanley Elam, Eds., *Values in American Education: An Interdisciplinary Approach* (Phi Delta Kappa, Bloomington, Indiana, 1964, 180 pp.); Michael Belok et al., Eds., *Approaches to Values in Education* (Wm. C. Brown, Dubuque, Iowa, 1966, 322 pp.); and Philip G. Smith, Ed., *Value Theory and Education* (University of Illinois Press, 1970). In Donald Arnstine's *Philosophy of Education: Learning and Schooling* (Harper and Row, 1967, 388 pp.) chs. 6, 7, and 8 are especially good on aesthetics and curiosity.

3

Contemporary Educational Theories

The word "theory" has two central meanings. It can refer to a hypothesis or set of hypotheses that have been verified by observation or experiment, as in the case of the theory of gravitation. It can also be a general synonym for systematic thinking or a set of coherent thoughts. As regards theory in the first sense, education awaits development; as regards theory in the second sense, education has harvested a veritable cornucopia.

In this chapter we shall explore four educational theories that lead or have led to programs of reform. Although these theories tend to flow from formal philosophies, they take on a special character because they are conditioned largely by experiences unique to education. Two other modes of thinking about education—existentialism and analysis—I will leave for separate treatment.

In this country the first educational theory to excite widespread attention was that of "Progressivism." The progressive movement, to be analyzed presently, burst upon the educational scene with revolutionary force. It called for the replacement of time-honored practices by a new kind of education based on social change and the findings of the behavioral sciences. The very force of the progressive movement and the publicity that it received paved the way for a counterrevolution. A revived conservatism decried the excesses of the progressivists, at the same time accepting some of their more moderate doctrines. This movement was known as "Perennialism." I will discuss it now because its fundamental themes antedated those of progressivism.

PERENNIALISM

Against the progressive emphasis on change and novelty, perennialists call for allegiance to absolute principles. Despite momentous social upheavals, permanence, they say, is more real than change. It is also more desirable as an ideal. In a world of increasing precariousness and uncertainty nothing can be more beneficial than steadfastness of educational purpose and stability in educational behavior.[1] The basic principles of perennialism may be outlined in six categories.

1. *Despite differing environments, human nature remains the same everywhere; hence, education should be the same for everyone.* "The function of a citizen or a subject," writes Robert M. Hutchins,

[1] Perennialism's philosophic foundations are embedded in classical realism; the philosophers most quoted are Aristotle and Aquinas. Among its leading spokesmen are Robert Maynard Hutchins, Mortimer J. Adler, and Sir Richard Livingstone, an English classicist who has won an appreciable following in the United States. Although some perennialist ideas are in practice nearly everywhere, they have been applied most consistently at St. John's College, Annapolis, Maryland.

". . . may vary from society to society . . . . But the function of a man, as a man, is the same in every age and in every society, since it results from his nature as a man. The aim of an educational system is the same in every age and in every society where such a system can exist: it is to improve man as man."[2]

Or, in Mortimer Adler's words,

"If a man is a rational animal, constant in nature throughout history, then there must be certain constant features in every sound educational program, regardless of culture or epoch."[3]

Knowledge, too, is everywhere the same. If it were not, learned men could never agree on anything. Opinion, of course, is different; here men may disagree. (But when they do agree, opinion becomes knowledge.) Admittedly, the acquisition of knowledge is not easy and some children are apt to resist it. Admittedly, too, some children take longer to learn than others. But this only means that we must spend more time with them. Are we not, asks the perennialist, fostering a false notion of equality when we promote children on the basis of age rather than intellectual attainment? Is it not likely that they will gain greater self-respect from knowing that they have *earned* promotion by passing the same tests as those given to other children of their age?

2. *Since rationality is man's highest attribute, he must use it to direct his instinctual nature in accordance with deliberately chosen ends.* Men are free, but they must learn to cultivate reason and control their appetites. When a child fails to learn, teachers should not be quick to place the blame on an unhappy environment or an unfortunate psychological train of events. Rather, the teacher's job is to overcome these handicaps through an essentially intellectual approach to learning that will be the same for all his pupils. Nor should teachers

---

[2] Robert Maynard Hutchins, *The Conflict in Education*, Harper, New York, 1953, p. 68.

[3] Mortimer J. Adler, "The Crisis in Contemporary Education," *The Social Frontier*, **V** (February 1939), 141-144 .

become permissive on the grounds that only thus may a child relieve his tensions and express his true self. No child should be permitted to determine his own educational experience, for what he wants may not be what he should have.

3. *It is education's task to import knowledge of eternal truth.* In Hutchins' celebrated but vulnerable deduction,

"Education implies teaching. Teaching implies knowledge. Knowledge is truth. The truth is everywhere the same. Hence, education should be everywhere the same."[4]

Education should seek to adjust the individual not to the world as such but to what is true. Adjustment to truth is the end of learning.

4. *Education is not an imitation of life but a preparation for it.* The school can never be a "real-life situation." Nor should it be; it remains for the child an artificial arrangement in which he becomes acquainted with the finest achievements of his cultural heritage. His task is to realize the values of this heritage and, where possible, add to its achievements through his own endeavors.

5. *The student should be taught certain basic subjects that will acquaint him with the world's permanencies.* He should not be hustled into studies that seem important at the time. Nor should he be allowed to learn what appeals to him at a particular age. He should study English, languages, history, mathematics, natural science, philosophy, and fine arts. "The basic education of a rational animal," writes Adler,

". . . is the discipline of his rational powers and the cultivation of his intellect. This discipline is achieved through the liberal arts, the arts of reading and listening, of writing and speaking, and, perforce, of thinking, since man is a social animal as well as a rational one and his intellectual life is lived in a community which can exist only through the communication

---

[4] Robert Maynard Hutchins, *The Higher Learning in America*, Yale University Press, New Haven, Conn., 1936, p. 66.

of men. The three R's, which always signified the formal disciplines, are the essence of liberal or general education."[5]

Vocational, industrial, and similar types of education may be included, provided their instruction is intellectually sound. However, the school does not exist to train for occupational tasks; these are best left to practitioners in the field. Nor should the school stump for social reform. Democracy will progress because people are properly educated and not because they have been taught to agitate for social change.

6. *Students should study the great works of literature, philosophy, history, and science in which men through the ages have revealed their greatest aspirations and achievements.* The message of the past is never dated. By examining it, the student learns truths that are more important than any he could find by pursuing his own interests or dipping into the contemporary scene. Mortimer Adler summarizes this view admirably:

"If there is philosophical wisdom as well as scientific knowledge, if the former consists of insights and ideas that change little from time to time, and if even the latter has many abiding concepts and a relatively constant method, if the great works of literature as well as of philosophy touch upon the permanent moral problems of mankind and express the universal convictions of men involved in moral conflict—if these things are so, then the great books of ancient and medieval, as well as modern times are a repository of knowledge and wisdom, a tradition of culture which must initiate each new generation. The reading of these books is not for antiquarian purposes; the interest is not archaeological or philological . . . . Rather the books are to be read because they are as contemporary today as when they were written, and that because the *problems they deal with and the ideas they present are not subject to the law of perpetual and interminable progress.*"[6]

In short, say the perennialists, the minds of most young Americans have never really been exercised in intellectual mat-

---

[5] Adler, op. cit., p. 62.
[6] Ibid., p. 63. Thus Adler expounds what has been called the "Great Books" Theory.

ters, largely because teachers themselves are indifferent and give up too quickly. It is much easier to teach students at their own pace and in accordance with what they want to learn. Yet, in allowing the child's superficial inclinations to determine what he learns, we may actually hinder him from developing his real talents. Self-realization demands self-discipline, and self-discipline is attained only through external discipline. Those higher interests—literary, artistic, political, and religious —one or more of which are latent in everyone, do not emerge without hard work and application. It is all too easy to underestimate the child's abilities in these directions. Why not make every man a king in some intellectual realm? This, surely, is a worthier goal than settling for intellectual mediocrity and falsely equating such mediocrity with individual freedom.

Critique of Perennialism

Perennialists may be accused of fostering an "aristocracy of intellect" and unreasonably restricting their teaching to the classical tradition of the Great Books. They fail to appreciate that, although many children lack the particular intellectual gifts perennialism emphasizes, they nevertheless become good citizens and productive workers. To subject them to the same sort of rigorous academic training as that given to students of university caliber is to ignore this difference and perhaps to injure their personal growth. Indeed, such practice actually may retard the development of attributes that are equally as valuable as any academic qualities they may have acquired in school. The intellect is only one side of a man's personality. And although rational behavior is indispensable to human progress, the affective and uniquely personal side can ill afford to be subordinated.[7]

---

[7] Many other criticisms may be leveled at perennialism, but they are inherent in the tenets of rival doctrines, as outlined in this chapter. On the matter of the sameness of human nature everywhere, however, I cannot refrain from citing a retort attributed to the anthropologist Clyde Kluckhohn: "Every man is in certain respects (a) like all other men, (b) like some other men, (c) like no other man."

PROGRESSIVISM

By the turn of the century a number of educators already had rebelled against the excessive formalism of traditional education, with its emphasis on strict discipline, passive learning, and pointless detail. As far back as the 1870s Francis W. Parker was advocating school reforms later to be revised and formalized by John Dewey. However, Dewey's first major work, *Schools of Tomorrow*, was not published until 1915, and another four years went by before the Progressive Education Association was founded. Thus, progressivism had been on the move for 30 years before its impact actually was felt. In its early stages it was largely individualist in temper, reflecting the bohemianism of the age; it was at this point that it attracted the support of William Heard Kilpatrick of Columbia University.

With the onset of the Depression in the 1930s, progressivism swung its weight behind a movement for social change, thus sacrificing its earlier emphasis on individual development and embracing such ideals as "cooperation," "sharing," and "adjustment." During this period it was joined by John L. Childs, George Counts, and Boyd H. Bode. The Progressive Education Association has long been disbanded, and the movement suffered a major reversal after the USSR launched its Sputnik,[8] but progressivism continues to exercise considerable influence through the individual work of such contemporaries as George Axtelle, William O. Stanley, Ernest Bayles, Lawrence G. Thomas, and Frederick C. Neff.

Taking the pragmatist view that change, not permanence, is

[8] Progressivism always attracted a lion's share of criticism, but never more so than during the days of mingled amazement and humiliation that followed the launching of the first Soviet sputnik. Americans had been convinced that Russian education was undemocratic and authoritarian and, therefore, ineffective. But how could such success in science and technology be explained? Could it be that American schools were paying too much attention to the children they taught and too little to the subjects they taught them? There was a revulsion against the "child-centeredness" identified with progressivism. Americans, it was said, had pandered to their children too long; the nation was going soft; the rot must be stopped.

the essence of reality, progressivism in its pure form declares that education is always in the process of development. Educators must be ready to modify methods and policies in the light of new knowledge and changes in the environment. The special quality of education is not to be determined by applying perennial standards of goodness, truth, and beauty, but by construing education as a *continual reconstruction of experience*. As Dewey expresses it,

"We thus reach a technical definition of education: it is that reconstruction or reorganization of experience which adds to the meaning of experience, and which increases the ability to direct the course of subsequent experience."[9]

Moreover, during the course of its development progressivism began to make some assertions of its own, six of which I will now discuss.

1. *Education should be life itself, not a preparation for living.* Intelligent living involves the interpretation and reconstruction of experience. The child should enter into learning situations suited to his age and oriented toward experiences that he is likely to undergo in adult life.

2. *Learning should be directly related to the interests of the child.* Progressive educators introduce the concept of the "whole child" as an answer to what they consider partial interpretations of the child's nature.[10] Thus Kilpatrick advocates the "child-centered" school, in which the process of learning is determined mainly by the individual child. A young person, he says, is naturally disposed to learn whatever relates to his interests or appears to solve his problems; at the same time,

---

[9] John Dewey, *Democracy and Education*, Macmillan, New York, 1916, p. 89.

[10] William Heard Kilpatrick, "The Essentials of the Activity Movement," *Progressive Education*, II (October 1934) 357-358: "The conception of 'the whole child' carries two implications which at bottom agree: one, that we wish at no time to disregard the varied aspects of child life; the other, that the child as an organism properly responds as one unified whole."

he naturally tends to resist whatever he feels to be imposed on him from above. The child, then, should learn because he needs and wants to learn, not necessarily because someone else thinks that he should. He should be able to see the relevance of what he learns to his own life and not to an adult's conception of the sort of life that a child of his age should be leading.

This does not mean that the child should be allowed to follow every prompting of his own desires, if only for the fact that he is not mature enough to define significant purposes. And although he may have much to do in determining the learning process, he is not its final arbiter. He needs guidance and direction from teachers who are equipped to perceive meaning in his discrete activities. The child experiences a continuous reconstruction of his private interests as they move to embrace the logical content of subject matter.[11]

Even so, the progressive teacher influences the growth of his pupils not by drumming bits of information into their heads but by controlling the environment in which growth takes place. Growth is defined as the "increase of intelligence in the management of life" and "intelligent adaptation to an environment." Dewey advised the teacher: "Now see to it that day by day the conditions are such that their own activities move inevitably in this direction, toward such culmination of themselves."[12]

3. *Learning through problem solving should take precedence over the inculcating of subject matter.* Progressivists reject the

[11] The view that the individual child should be the center of the school's activity is much older than the writings of either Dewey or the progressivists. It was advocated, for varying philosophical reasons, by Rousseau, Froebel, Pestalozzi, Francis Parker, and G. Stanley Hall. However, it underwent a radical shift in meaning within the context of the moral relativism advanced by the progressive movement. When Froebel, for instance, argued for the free unfolding of the child's nature, he did so with an absolute goal in mind —that of allowing the child to unite himself spontaneously with God under the inspired guidance of his teacher. Progressivism acknowledges no absolute goal, unless it is social progress attained through individual freedom.

[12] John Dewey, *The Child and the Curriculum*, University of Chicago, Chicago, Ill., 1943, p. 31.

view that learning consists essentially of the reception of knowledge and that knowledge itself is an abstract substance that the teacher loads into the minds of his pupils. Knowledge, they declare, is a "tool for managing experience," for handling the continuously novel situations with which the mutability of life confronts us. If knowledge is to be significant, we must be able to do something with it; hence, it must be wedded to experience. Dewey says that we have learned all this from experimental science:

"The most direct blow at the traditional separation of doing and knowing and at the traditional prestige of purely 'intellectual' studies, however, has been given by the progress of experimental science. If this progress has demonstrated anything, it is that there is no such thing as genuine knowledge and fruitful understanding except as the offspring of doing . . . . Men have *to do* something to the things when they wish to find out something; they have to alter conditions. This is the lesson of the laboratory method, and the lesson which all education has to learn."[13]

Thus, the search for abstract knowledge must be translated into an active educational experience. If the student is to gain any real appreciation of social and political ideas, the classroom itself must become a living experiment in social democracy. Indeed, experience and experiment are the key words of the progressivist method of learning. Dewey does not reject the content of traditional subject matter; on the contrary, he insists that much of it be retained. But, he says, subject matter constantly changes in terms of what men do with their environment. Consequently, education cannot be limited to a recollection of information obtained solely from a teacher or a textbook. It is not the absorption of previous knowledge that counts but its constant reconstruction in the light of new discoveries. Thus, problem solving must be seen not as the search for merely functional knowledge, but as a "perpetual grappling" with subject matter. Grappling is to be understood not

[13] Dewey, *Democracy and Education*, op. cit., pp. 321-322.

only as physical motion, that is, handling test tubes, or counting money, or raising one's hand to vote, but also as critical thinking, reconstruction of previously held ideas, and discovery.

Instead of teaching formal subject matter, we should substitute specific problem areas such as transportation, communication, and trade. But not even these can be fixed too far in advance. "Thus a curriculum," declares Lawrence G. Thomas,

". . . cannot be more than outlined broadly in advance by the teacher and will consist largely of an array of resources which the teacher anticipates may be called upon as the current activities of the class lead on to new interests and new problems. The actual details of the curriculum must be constructed cooperatively in the classroom from week to week."[14]

Kilpatrick suggests that, instead of trying to grasp abstract principles on a theoretical level, the child should study particular topics or situations, such as Galileo's method of experimentation or the way in which the Hopi Indians gather and prepare food. The purpose is to enable the student to cope with his own problems by observing how others have done so elsewhere and at other times. The student engages in projects that (a) spring from his natural curiosity to learn and (b) acquire significance as they are worked out in cooperation with other members of the class and under the guidance of the teacher. Thus, all projects should be both personally and socially significant.

4. *The teacher's role is not to direct but to advise.* Because their own needs and desires determine what they learn, children should be allowed to plan their own development and the teacher should guide the learning involved. He should employ his greater knowledge and experience to help them whenever they reach an impasse. Without directing the course of events, he works with the children for the attainment of

---

[14] Lawrence G. Thomas, "The Meaning of 'Progress' to Progressive Education," *Educational Administration and Supervision,* **XXXII**, 7 (October, 1946), 399.

mutually agreeable ends. "In the Progressive view," declares Lawrence G. Thomas,

". . . the teacher merely has superior and richer experience to bring to bear on the analysis of the present situation . . . . The teacher is vitally important as stage setter, guide, and co-ordinator, but he is not the sole source of authority."[15]

5. *The school should encourage cooperation rather than competition.* Men are social by nature and derive their greatest satisfaction from their relations with one another. Progressivists maintain that love and partnership are more appropriate to education than competition and personal gain. Thus education as the "reconstruction of experience" leads to the "reconstruction of human nature" in a social setting. The progressivist does not deny that competition has a certain value. He agrees that students should compete with one another, provided that such competition fosters personal growth. Nevertheless, he insists that cooperation is better suited than competition to the biological and social facts of human nature. Rugged individualism is permissible only when it serves the general good.[16]

6. *Only democracy permits—indeed encourages—the free interplay of ideas and personalities that is a necessary condition of true growth.* Principles 5 and 6 are interrelated, because in the progressivist view democracy and cooperation are said to imply each other. Ideally democracy is "shared experience." As Dewey puts it, "A democracy is more than a form of government; it is primarily a mode of associated living, of conjoint communicated experience." Democracy, growth, and educa-

---

[15] Ibid., p. 398.

[16] Progressivism rejects the social Darwinist view, developed by Herbert Spencer, that society should imitate nature and encourage competition. Life in the jungle does indeed appear "red in tooth and claw," but only when animals are hungry, angered, or mating. Even if nature did possess the characteristics imputed to it by social Darwinism, the argument that since ruthlessness is present in nature, it is therefore desirable in society, would still be untenable. Because they are unable to control their condition, animals cannot improve it; man, who is, can.

tion are thus interrelated. In order to teach democracy, the school itself must be democratic. It should promote student government, the free discussion of ideas, joint pupil-staff planning, and the full participation of all in the educative experience. However, schools should not indoctrinate students in the tenets of a new social order. To instruct them in a specific program of social and political action would be to adopt an authoritarianism that progressivism specifically rejects.

Critique of Progressivism

I have already stated that some of Dewey's followers carried his teachings to lengths he himself never intended. This is particularly true of his "doctrine of interest." One result was the much criticized "child-activity movement" that flourished during the 1930s and 1940s. Self-activity may well lead to individual improvement, social betterment, and the good life. But how are "improvement," "betterment," and "the good life" to be defined? If the child is to be permitted freedom for self-activity, there should be a fixed goal for him to attain. The conception of child activity admirably illustrates the progressivist theory that growth should lead to more growth. Yet the entire process seems circular in nature. Growth as such cannot be self-justifying, for we need to know to what end it is directed. We require the assurance that, when we strive to achieve a certain goal, it will be desirable in itself when we actually attain it and not liable to replacement by another goal.

The progressivist has good psychological grounds for his claim that the child is not a little adult and that he must not be treated simply as a scholar. Rousseau was one of the first to call this fact to our attention. He also stated that it was useless to expect a child to indulge in abstract intellectual pursuits until he had reached the age of reason. Instead, a child should learn the things he is capable of understanding through personal discovery. However, his life displays many features, not the least of which is a process of intellectual growth and change. Is it not risky, therefore, to allow the child's interests so great an influence over what he learns? Viewed in retrospect, today's interests may seem as dull as yesterday's newspaper. How far should we give way to the child's desire to be a cowboy? How far should we encourage his desire to shoot Indians? Progressivists themselves are aware of the dangers of too great an emphasis on "presentism" in educational practice. Boyd Bode points out that the school should lead the child not merely to live but also to "transcend" his immediate existence and outgrow any habit that might keep him immature. It is part of the intelligent life, and therefore of education itself, to heed the demands of the future as well as those of the present.

It is also difficult to see how the school could be a replica of life, even if it tried. Inevitably the school is an artificial learning situation, beset with restrictions and prohibitions different from those encountered in life as a whole. Not only is it simply one life situation, it is also only one educational agency. It assumes tasks that other social agencies cannot handle. Indeed, the logic of the progressivist leads him to an odd dilemma. On the one hand, he advocates a real-life situation; on the other, he calls for types of tolerance, freedom, and control rarely permitted by the stern exigencies of life.

Progressivists claim that learning through problem solving leads to more genuine intellectual attainment than do other methods of learning. But this claim cannot be verified. Protagonists point to such experiments as the Eight-Year Study of 1933 to show that students who have been prepared for college by progressive methods do as well as, or better than, those prepared in the traditional way.[17] But the study is not definitive. Critics insist that the number of uncontrolled variables in the experiment nullifies its validity. Even so, Dewey did not intend that learning should remain indefinitely at the level of problem solving. On the contrary, problem solving is a means by which the child is led from practical issues to theoretical

---

[17] W. Aiken, *The Story of the Eight-Year Study*, Harper, New York, 1942. Aiken concluded that what was important was not the type or number of subjects studied but the quality of the work done.

principles, from the concrete and sensory to the abstract and intellectual.[18]

The progressivist cites in his defense the fact that education culminates at the graduate level, where the professor acts more as a resource person than as a dictator of studies. Although graduate education permits the student considerable personal freedom, it is debatable whether elementary and secondary education should adopt the same procedure. We allow graduate students this freedom because they are intellectually mature and presumably can recognize where their true interests lie. The progressivist could reply that his methods of learning accustom the child to independent research and self-reliance from the very beginning of his school career; they enable him to reach this intellectual maturity earlier than he is permitted to at present. The core of the dispute reduces itself to the question of how far the self-discipline necessary to intellectual maturity can be self-taught and how far it should be developed through external discipline. However, since the ability to discriminate between essential and nonessential knowledge is largely an adult achievement, it would seem that the teacher himself should impart the bulk of what the child learns.

On the matter of cooperation as opposed to competition I will mention only one point. The individual wishing to contribute to the general good may on occasion be unable to cooperate, precisely because his ideals and life style are unacceptable to the group. The tyranny of the group has dangers of its own; it is not necessarily more clear-headed than the individual. The mass mind at times may wear moral and intel-

---

[18] Cf. Foster McMurray, "The Present Status of Pragmatism in Education," *School and Society*, **LXXXVII** (2145) (January 17, 1959), 14-15: "Clearly the intent of Dewey's theory was to stimulate more and better learning of arts, sciences, and technologies. There was in this program no concern for immediate practical or directly utilitarian bits of information and technique, nor any process of choosing and organizing information around characteristic activities of daily life. On the contrary, in Dewey's version of pragmatism, characteristic activities of daily life were psychologically useful starting points for moving the learner to a consideration of meaning increasingly remote, abstract, and related to one another in impersonal systems rather than to practical daily use."

lectual blinders that a single mind does not. We must therefore make sure that our cooperation is free and unforced—in short, that it does not become conformism.

Finally, Dewey's definition of democracy may be more comprehensive than most; nevertheless, although his theory of democracy leads him to certain conclusions about behavior in the school, other doctrines are equally democratic. Until recently French education has been authoritarian (judged by progressivist standards), but France is surely a democracy, and her educational system corresponds to the wishes of the majority of her people. Perennialism, which has been criticized as reactionary and antidemocratic, is committed just as firmly to democracy as is progressivism. Indeed, it would be difficult to find a more vigorous defender of the democratic way of life than Robert M. Hutchins. The point is that different thinkers advance different interpretations of the democratic way of life; all of them are permissible, but none is definitive. American democracy has room for all sorts of responsible educational ideas.

Even so, progressivism has introduced many worthwhile reforms into American education, reforms that other outlooks must consider if they wish to retain their influence. By drawing attention to the currents of change and renewal that run constantly through the universe and through education itself, and by continually challenging the existing order, progressivism expresses an educational attitude of abiding significance.

ESSENTIALISM

Essentialism is not linked formally to any philosophic tradition, but is compatible with a variety of philosophic outlooks. Unlike perennialism, some of whose views it rejects, it is not opposed to progressivism as a whole but only to specific aspects. In maintaining that there are certain essentials that all men should know if they are to be considered educated, it does not repudiate Dewey's epistemology so much as the pronouncements of his less cautious followers. The essentialists devote their main efforts to (a) reexamining curricular matters, (b) distinguishing the essential and the nonessential in school programs, and (c) reestablishing the authority of the teacher in the classroom.

Founded in the early 1930s, the essentialist movement included such educators as William C. Bagley, Thomas Briggs, Frederick Breed, and Isaac L. Kandel. It also won the support of Herman H. Horne. In 1938, these men formed the Essentialist Committee for the Advancement of American Education. The tradition continues in the writings of William Brickman, editor of *School and Society*. The Council for Basic Education, whose most active members are Arthur Bestor and Mortimer Smith, may also be considered essentialist in spirit, although members are skeptical of the value of formal educational studies by specialists in education. In fact, they say, the "educational establishment," consisting chiefly of schools and professors of education, is largely responsible for what they believe to be the sorry state of American education today.[19]

Like perennialism, essentialism stands for the reinstatement of subject matter at the center of the educational process. However, it does not share the perennialist's view that the true subject matter of education is the "eternal verities" preserved in the "great books" of Western civilization. These books should be used, but not for themselves. They should be made to relate to present realities.

---

[19] Critics of education as a formal study usually advocate that "what little there is of it" should be incorporated into other disciplines. The philosophy of education, then, would be taught by professors of philosophy in the department of philosophy; the history of education would be handled in a department of history; and so on. But why stop with education? The philosophy of science, of history, of politics, etc., by this reasoning, would all be taught in a philosophy department. Indeed, since all subjects are usually taught in English, why not deal with them all in an English department? Conversely, since all disciplines are educational, why not teach them all in a department of education? Bestor, a historian, would substantially reduce the number of professional courses taken by student teachers and curtail the influence of educationists on the practice of education. Brickman, an educationist, calls for more data and fewer polemics from writers such as Bestor who, in his view, are not qualified to make responsible judgments about a field as complex as education.

Some essentialists turn to educational psychology for knowledge about the process of learning and the nature of the learner. Others are less confident. Although not denying the relevance to education of the findings of the behavioral sciences, they nevertheless view them more critically. In a field such as psychology, where little is claimed that is not instantly disputed, the educator, they say, would be wise to tread cautiously. Field theory conflicts with behaviorism and functionalism with psychoanalysis, so that it is impossible to tell which provides the more reliable knowledge. Until the findings of educational psychology become more genuinely scientific, some essentialists will regard them with considerable skepticism.

Essentialists have no united front. Since they hold different philosophies, it is not surprising that they disagree on the ultimate nature and value of education. Agreement is reached, however, on four fundamental principles.

1. *Learning, of its very nature, involves hard work and often unwilling application.* The essentialist insists on the importance of discipline. Instead of stressing the child's immediate interests, he urges dedication to more distant goals. Against the progressive emphasis on personal interest, he posits the concept of effort. He agrees that interest in a subject does much to create the effort needed to master it, but points out that higher and more enduring interests are not normally felt at the outset; they arise through hard work from beginnings that do not in themselves attract the learner. Thus, the command of a foreign language, once attained, opens new worlds for the mind; yet the beginner often must overcome initial apathy and probable distaste. As the Frenchman says, "The appetite comes while eating."

Among living things man alone can resist his immediate impulses. If we do not encourage this capacity in the child, we make it harder for him to attain self-discipline necessary to achieve any worthwhile end. The vast majority of students attain personal control only through voluntary submission to discipline intelligently imposed by the teacher.

2. *The initiative in education should lie with the teacher rather than with the pupil.* The teacher's role is to mediate between the adult world and the world of the child. The teacher has been specially prepared for this task and is, therefore, much better qualified to guide the growth of his pupils than they are themselves. Isaac L. Kandel maintains that:

"The essentialist is no less interested than the progressive in the principle that learning cannot be successful unless it is based on the capacities, interests, and purpose of the learner, but he believes those interests and purposes must be made over by the skill of the teacher, who is master of that 'logical organization' called subjects and who understands the process of educational developments."[20]

Thus, the essentialist teacher wields greater authority than does his progressivist colleague.[21]

3. *The heart of the educational process is the assimilation of prescribed subject matter.* This view accords with the philosophic realist's position that it is largely man's material and social environment that dictates how he shall live. The essentialist agrees that education should enable the individual to realize his potentialities, but such realization must take place in a world independent of the individual—a world whose laws he must obey. The purpose of the child's attending school is to get to know this world as it really is and not to interpret it in the light of his own peculiar desires. Nor can he assimilate such knowledge haphazardly in whatever order he likes. It

[20] Quoted by William W. Brickman, "Essentialism—Ten Years After," *School and Society,* **XLVII** (May 15, 1948), 365.

[21] William W. Brickman, "The Essentialist Spirit in Education," *School and Society,* **LXXXVI** (October 11, 1958), 364: "Essentialism places the teacher at the center of the educational universe. This teacher must have a liberal education, a scholarly knowledge of the field of learning, a deep understanding of the psychology of children and of the learning process, an ability to impart facts and ideals to the younger generation, an application of the historical-philosophical foundations of education, and a serious devotion to his work."

must be presented to him in accordance with the logical organization of subject matter (see pp. 88-89).[22]

Essentialists emphasize the importance of "race experience" —the "social heritage"—over the experience of the individual. This heritage summarizes the experiences of millions in attempting to come to terms with their environment. The wisdom of the many, tested by history, is far more reliable than the untested experience of the child.

4. *The school should retain traditional methods of mental discipline.* There are, it is true, certain advantages to the progressive method of problem solving, but it is not a procedure to be applied throughout the entire learning process. Of its very nature, much knowledge is abstract and cannot be broken up into discrete problems.

Although "learning by doing" may be appropriate in certain circumstances and for certain children, it should not be generalized. Must the child actually build a wigwam in order to learn how the Indian becomes domesticated? There is no doubt that doing so will help him to understand the Indian's way of life, but such an experience should support the learning process rather than constitute its essence. The child should be taught essential concepts, even if such concepts have to be adapted to his own psychological and intellectual level.

How does essentialism differ from perennialism? First, it advocates a less totally "intellectual" education, for it is concerned not so much with certain supposedly eternal truths as with the adjustment of the individual to his physical and social environment. Second, it is more willing to absorb the positive contributions that progressivism has made to educational methods. Finally, where perennialism reveres the great creative achievements of the past as timeless expressions of

[22] Isaac L. Kandel, *Conflicting Theories of Education*, Macmillan, New York, 1938, p. 99: "Since the environment carries in itself the stamp of the past and the seeds of the future, the curriculum must inevitably include that knowledge and information which will acquaint the pupil with the social heritage, introduce him to the world about him, and prepare him for the future."

man's universal insights, essentialism uses them as sources of knowledge for dealing with problems of the present.[23]

RECONSTRUCTIONISM

As far back as 1920 John Dewey suggested the term "reconstructionism" in the title of his book, *Reconstruction in Philosophy*. In the early 1930s, a group known as the "Frontier Thinkers" called on the school to lead the way toward the creation of a "new" and "more equitable" society. Their leading spokesmen were George Counts and Harold Rugg. Counts had written *The American Road to Culture* (1930) and *Dare the Schools Build a New Social Order?* (1932), and Rugg had published *Culture and Education in America* (1931). At this time progressivists such as W. H. Kilpatrick and John Childs were also urging education to become more aware of its social responsibilities. But they disagreed with the contention of Counts and Rugg that the school should commit itself to specific social reforms; they preferred instead to stress the general end of social growth through education.

Two decades later, as the progressive movement lost its momentum, further attempts were made to extend Deweyan philosophy into socially committed educational theories. In his major work, *The Ideal and the Community* (1958), Isaac B. Berkson sought a *rapprochement* of progressivism and essentialism, suggesting that although the school itself should not

[23] Most attacks made on public education in the United States are likely to be essentialist in nature. The criticism of commentators such as Paul Woodring and James B. Conant is more conciliatory and could be placed halfway between the progressive and the essentialist points of view. Admiral Hyman G. Rickover, although not a professional educator, has affinities with both essentialism and perennialism. Like many essentialists, he esteems the contributions made to educational practice by the physical sciences more highly than he does those made by the behavioral sciences. He advocates more emphasis on knowledge for its own sake. Speaking as a professor of History, Jacques Barzun leans toward perennialism rather than essentialism, largely because he places the humanities at the center of the curriculum and believes in studying them for their own sake.

take the lead in social reform, it could cooperate with movements already underway that advocated a more thorough realization of liberal cultural values. However, it was Theodore Brameld who laid the foundations of "social reconstructionism" with the publication of *Patterns of Educational Philosophy* (1950), followed by *Toward a Reconstructed Philosophy of Education* (1956) and *Education as Power* (1965).[24] My resumé of reconstructionism will be limited to five of the main theses that Brameld puts forward.

1. *Education must commit itself here and now to the creation of a new social order that will fulfill the basic values of our culture and at the same time harmonize with the underlying social and economic forces of the modern world.* Claiming to be the philosophy of an "age in crisis," reconstructionism sounds a note of urgency not heard in other educational theories. Civilization, it declares, now faces the possibility of self-annihilation. Education must lead to a profound change in the minds of men, so that the enormous technological power at our disposal may be used to create rather than to destroy. Society must be transformed, not simply through political action, but more fundamentally through the education of its members to a new vision of their life in common. This commitment to the new order is not tenuous but urgent and direct. Reconstructionism, writes Brameld,

". . . commits itself, first of all, to the building of a new culture. It is infused with a profound conviction that we are in the midst of a revolutionary period out of which would emerge nothing less than control of the industrial system, of public services, and of cultural and natural resources by and for the common people who, throughout the ages, have strug-

[24] In his *Patterns of Educational Philosophy*, World Book, Yonkers, N.Y., 1950, p. 204, Brameld criticizes progressivism as "dilatory" and "inefficient." It is, he says, "the educational effort of an adolescent culture, suffering from the pleasant agonies of growing up, from the cultural period of trying and erring when the protections of infancy have been left behind but the planned autonomies of maturity await future delineation and fulfillment."

gled for a life of security, decency, and peace for them and their children."[25]

2. *The new society must be a genuine democracy, whose major institutions and resources are controlled by the people themselves.* Anything that sufficiently affects the public interest, whether pensions, health, or industry, should become the responsibility of elected popular representatives. Thus Brameld declares:

"Control by the largest possible majority of the principal institutions and resources of any culture is the supreme test of democracy . . . the working people should control all principal institutions and resources if the world is to become genuinely democratic."[26]

Since the ideal society is a democracy, it must also be realized democratically. The structure, goals, and policies of the new order must be approved at the bar of public opinion and enacted with the fullest possible measure of popular support. A revolution that takes place in the minds of a people is more profound and lasting than any change brought about by politicians alone. And the logical end of national democracy is international democracy, a form of world government in which all states will participate.[27]

[25] Theodore Brameld, "Philosophies of Education in an Age of Crisis," *School and Society*, **LXV** (June 21, 1947), 452.

[26] Theodore Brameld, *Toward a Reconstructed Philosophy of Education*, Dryden, New York, 1956, pp. 328-329.

[27] Theodore Brameld, *Education as Power*, Holt, Rinehart and Winston, New York, 1965, p. 6: "The majority of peoples should, through their freely chosen representatives, control all fundamental economic, political, and social policies, and they should do so on a planetary scale. This is the supreme goal of education for the current decades. As long as our schools avoid recognition of this purpose; as long as teachers and professors skirt the subject because it is controversial; as long as educational theorists say, 'Oh, no, we must be concerned with training mental faculties,' or 'We must support the power struggle to glorious victory for our side,' then they are, in my judgment, denying a central purpose of education. To find a way to enlist and unite the majority of peoples of all races, religions, and nationalities into a great democratic world body with power and authority to enforce its policies—what greater mandate to us in the profession of education can be imagined than this?"

3. *The child, the school, and education itself are conditioned inexorably by social and cultural forces.* Progressivism, says Brameld, overstates the case for individual freedom and understates the extent to which we are all socially conditioned. In its concern to find ways in which the individual may realize himself in society, it overlooks the degree to which society makes him what he is. Since civilized life by and large is group life, groups should play an important part in the school. "We should recognize groups for what they are," writes Brameld, "We should neither cynically condemn them nor passively accept their behavior as inevitable, but through sound diagnosis aim to build a social and educational program that will help resolve their longings, reduce their immoralities, and release their humane potentialities."[28] Thus education becomes "social self-realization"; through it the individual not only develops the social side of his nature but also learns how to participate in social planning.

4. *The teacher must convince his pupils of the validity and urgency of the reconstructionist solution, but he must do so with scrupulous regard for democratic procedures.* Under what Brameld calls the principle of "defensible partiality," the teacher allows open examination of the evidence both for and against his views; he presents alternative solutions fairly; and he permits his pupils to defend their own ideas. Moreover, since all of us have convictions and partialities, we should not only express and defend them publicly but also "work for their acceptance by the largest possible majority."

5. *The means and ends of education must be completely refashioned to meet the demands of the present cultural crisis and to accord with the findings of the behavioral sciences.* The importance of the behavioral sciences is that they enable us to discover those values in which men most strongly believe, whether or not these values are universal. Thus, Brameld declares.

". . . the behavioral sciences are beginning to prove, really for the first time in history, that it is possible to formulate

[28] Theodore Brameld, *Patterns of Educational Philosophy*, World Book, Yonkers, N.Y., 1950, p. 425.

human goals not for sentimental, romantic, mystical, or similarly arbitrary reasons, but on the basis of what we are learning about cross-cultural and even universal values. Though studies in this difficult field have moved only a little way, they have moved far enough so that it is already becoming plausible both to describe these values objectively and to demonstrate that most human beings prefer them to alternative values."[29]

We must look afresh at the way in which our curricula are drawn up, the subjects they contain, the methods that are used, the structure of administration, and the ways in which teachers are trained. These must then be reconstructed in accordance with a unified theory of human nature, rationally and scientifically derived. It follows that we must construct a curriculum whose subjects and subdivisions are related integrally rather than treated as a sequence of knowledge components:

"A theory of unified man, both derived from and contributing to our experimental knowledge of human behavior in its multiple perspectives, not only should integrate all other fields of knowledge; it should provide them with a fresh and potent significance."[30]

Critique of Reconstructionism

Reconstructionism is stirringly expressed. Its appeal is all the more compelling because it claims to be based on reliable findings in the behavioral sciences. Such a claim, if true, would be difficult to counter. Unfortunately it is vitiated by the fact that these findings permit a variety of interpretations, of which Brameld's is only one. As has already been pointed out and as Brameld himself admits, the established empirical conclusions of the behavioral sciences are scant indeed, and they carry no certain implications for education. There are, in addition, as many disagreements among behavioral scientists as there are

[29] Theodore Brameld, "Imperatives for a Reconstructed Philosophy of Education," *School and Society*, **LXXXVII** (January 17, 1959), 20.
[30] Ibid.

among educators—and those, surely, are enough. What one sociologist or economist holds to be true is easily refuted by another; and psychologists do not agree about the kinds of behavior that are basic to a planned society. Science has yet to answer such questions as: What are the best values for men to accept? What social institutions best aid their realization? The boast of reconstructionism—that it is based on reliable scientific knowledge of human behavior—cannot be sustained.

Whether reconstructionism is as squarely in the mainstream of the American cultural tradition as its supporters claim is likewise open to doubt. Actually, liberal individualism is just as much a part of our tradition as is the commitment to democratically determined social ideals. It is difficult, indeed, to envisage a democracy as pluralist as the United States coming to any agreement on the far-reaching changes suggested by reconstructionists. It is one thing to vote yes or no for a political candidate or a bond issue but quite another to do so on the issues of education, affected, as they are, by a host of moral, religious, aesthetic, and social—not to mention personal—considerations. How could the many competing interests in American society find a national educational system that pleased them all?

Perhaps the kind of permissive indoctrination that Brameld advocates is really a contradiction in terms. Reconstructionism as a doctrine demands commitment; a reconstructionist teacher cannot teach the doctrine without being committed to it himself and without hoping to commit his students also. However hard he may try to attain detachment in the classroom, he cannot, in the nature of things, be both scientifically detached and ideologically involved. Inasmuch as our society is deeply divided over social values, nothing less than capitulation to a totalitarian movement is ever likely to unite it. Our entire political structure would have to change, and individual enterprise would be severely enfeebled. In my view, reconstructionism seems to lead to a collectivist society, in which men would believe anything to be true provided it was attained by scientific methods and accepted through informed social consensus when persuasively presented.

References

For recent publications on contemporary educational theories, see Frederick C. Neff, *Philosophy and American Education* (The Center for Applied Research in Education, New York, 1966, 168 pp.); and G. Max Wingo, *The Philosophy of American Education* (D. C. Heath, 1965, 438 pp.). These two volumes use the "schools of philosophy" approach. John P. Wynne's *Theories of Education* (Harper and Row, 1963, 521 pp.) is an imposing study of educational theory in all its historical, philosophic, social, and scientific dimensions. (Wynne says it took him thirty years to write the book, and I can believe it.) Of the many anthologies available, I will mention three: Joe Park, Ed., *Selected Readings in the Philosophy of Education* (Macmillan, 1968, 433 pp.); John Martin Rich, Ed., *Readings in the Philosophy of Education* (Wadsworth, 1966, 393 pp.); and Van Cleve Morris, Ed., *Modern Movements in Educational Philosophy* (Houghton Mifflin, 1969, 381 pp.). Like Wingo and Neff, Park structures his text according to schools of philosophy, whereas Rich and Morris use a topical or problems approach. Although Rich includes valuable discussion questions, his book suffers from the absence of bibliographies and an index.

4

The Challenge
of Existentialism

Most traditional philosophies have been of two kinds, meta-physical and skeptical. Metaphysical philosophies seek to explain certain fundamental features of experience by arguing that they derive from some further reality that this experience does not affect. Skeptical philosophies maintain that, since all human experience is deceptive, nothing can be known for certain and all metaphysical conceptions are provisional. Existentialism rejects both these courses. It argues against skepticism by claiming that men can discover the fundamental truths of their own existence. Against traditional metaphysics it argues that the real is what we experience. Reality, it claims, is *lived* reality. To describe the real we must describe not what is beyond but what is *in* the human condition.

Existentialism also differs *stylistically* from traditional philosophy. Because it is concerned with lived reality and with states of feeling in which this reality is fully apprehended, existentialist philosophy is generally more personal in style than traditional philosophy, being closer, in fact, to literature. I do not mean by this that existentialist philosophy is either less technical or more elegant than traditional philosophy. Martin Heidegger and Jean-Paul Sartre are highly technical philosophers, and Heidegger certainly is no model of clarity. Nevertheless, each writes in a personal and literary way, for each seeks to convey states of feeling as well as arguments, and each has forged a highly charged prose that is unmistakably his own.

I must also mention that existentialist philosophers have written little on education as such. Martin Buber is an exception. Gabriel Marcel frequently refers to education in passing. Jean-Paul Sartre has defined the educational significance of literature. Karl Jaspers has published a book on *The Idea of the University*. And Friedrich Nietzsche wrote a polemical essay on educational institutions that is radical and caustic enough to be relevant in our own day. This neglect of education is surprising when one considers how many traditional philosophers, such as Plato, Locke, Kant, and Dewey, have addressed themselves to educational problems. It becomes all the more surprising when one reflects that as a philosophy of personal life, existentialism is bound to yield insights into education, a process in which persons can either be made or make themselves. Perhaps the explanation is that a new school of thought is almost bound to concentrate on the theoretical problems it has raised and to leave till later or to others the application of its principles in realms where thought and practice converge, such as politics, law, and education. Be that as it may, the opportunity is all the greater for educators themselves to explore and synthesize the educational insights with which existentialism abounds. To do this, we must approach the doctrine on its own terms and attend to those themes with which it is most concerned.

THE WORLD VIEW

Existentialism springs from the iconoclastic works of the Danish philosopher, Soren Kierkegaard (1813-1855) and the German thinker Friedrich W. Nietzsche (1844-1900). Both men turned against ecclesiastical Christianity and the speculative philosophy of Hegel. Kierkegaard strove to revitalize Christianity from within, whereas Nietzsche denounced the otherworldliness of Christianity and advocated the yea-saying morality of the superman. The leading existentialists of our time are Martin Heidegger, Jean-Paul Sartre, Karl Jaspers, and Maurice Merleau-Ponty. Other existentialists are Gabriel Marcel and Paul Tillich, both Christian, and Martin Buber, Jewish.

Existentialists reject the traditional view that philosophy should be calm and detached above all. Philosophy, they say, should be reason *informed by passion*, because it is in passion, in states of heightened feeling, that ultimate realities are disclosed. Passionate reason is not unreason but the reason of the whole man. It is reason at grips with those fundamental realities of freedom, death, and other people with which human beings must contend. It is the opposite of dispassionate calculation, which manipulates abstractions and ignores the human predicament.[1]

For existentialism the physical universe, the world apart from man, has neither meaning nor purpose. It is a contingency, something that happens to be there. This is not to say that it is capricious. The regularities discovered by science are genuine enough. But they have no direct human significance. Understood properly, they correspond to no human ideals or desires save the desire for security, which is the desire to escape from the true freedom and the true terror of the human condition. In the universe man happens by chance. There is no

---

[1] For Heidegger, philosophy begins and ends not in reason or logic but *wonder*: "Wonder pervades and maintains it. . . . Logic is only one explanation of the way we think. . . . 'Exact' thinking is never the strictest thinking . . . it is limited to the mere calculation of what-is and ministers to this alone" (*What is Philosophy?*, Twayne, New York, 1958, pp. 83-85).

world order, no natural scheme of things, into which he is born. A man therefore owes nothing to nature but his existence. His existence, then, precedes his essence, in the sense that he must exist if he is to be anything at all. But existence does not make him. Existing, he makes himself. As Sartre has said:

"What is meant here by saying that existence precedes essence? It means that, first of all, man exists, turns up, appears on the scene and, only afterwards defines himself. If man, as the existentialist sees him, is indefinable, it is because at first he is nothing. Only afterwards will he be something and he himself will have made what he will be. . . . Not only is man what he conceives himself to be, but he is also what he wills himself to be after this thrust toward existence. Man is nothing other than what he makes himself."[2]

What a man becomes is his own responsibility. Either he makes himself or, in a sense, he allows himself to be made by others. He chooses what he will be (his "essence") or, again in a sense, allows it to be chosen for him. But in either case he chooses, for acquiescence is not choice renounced but weak choice. Acquiescence is the unavailing flight from freedom. A man who is made by others is still the author of himself, for he chooses to be what they make him. He is, one might say, manufactured by choice.

If we accept this world view, what follows? As free men and free teachers we must seek to expose and combat all those forces in culture and society that tend to dehumanize men by denying their freedom. We must repudiate the subordination of the person to economic "laws," the tyranny of the majority over the dissenting minority, and the stifling of individuality by social conformism.[3] We must urge our students to recog-

[2] Jean-Paul Sartre, *Existentialism*, Philosophical Library, New York, 1947, p. 18.

[3] Cf. Kierkegaard ("Concluding Unscientific Postscript" and "The Individual"): "A Crowd . . . in its very concept is the untruth . . . it renders the individual completely impenitent and irresponsible, or at least weakens his sense of responsibility by reducing it to a fraction. . . . Thereof was Christ

nize and fulfill the freedom that is theirs as persons. What we urge we must also practice by respecting their freedom as we value our own.

CHOOSING

In itself freedom is neither a goal nor an ideal. It is the *potential for action*.[4] I am what I *do*. My character is the sum of my own actions and it is therefore self-created. My character can change because I can always act differently. My destiny is my own. Freedom, therefore, is "dreadful," for I am responsible for what I become.[5] The drunkard, the neurotic, the drug addict, the man in a rut, the man at the end of his tether, you and I, all of us have made ourselves and can make ourselves again.

I am free, therefore I become. When I choose, I throw myself into the future, I make myself other than I am. I "ex-ist." I summon into being that which was mere possibility. I am *homo viator*, the self forever in transit.

The moment for choice is important. As Kierkegaard says, "There is danger afoot" (*Either/Or*). I may lose my nerve and choose wrongly, or I may fail to see the opportunity and so let circumstances take their way. Choose I must and choose In

---

crucified because, although He addressed himself to all, He would have no dealings with the crowd. . . . He would not found a party, did not permit balloting, but would be that He is, the Truth, which relates itself to the individual."

[4] No one expresses this view more passionately and pointedly than Martin Buber (*Between Man and Man*, Macmillan, New York, 1965, pp. 91-92): "Freedom—I love its flashing face. . . . I am devoted to it. I am always ready to join in the fight for it. . . . I give my left hand to the rebel and my right to the heretic: Forward! But I do not trust them. They know how to die, but that is not enough. . . . They must not make freedom into a theorem or a program. To become free of a bond is destiny; one carries that like a cross, not like a cockade. . . . Life lived in freedom is *personal* responsibility."

[5] In Sartre's *The Flies*, Orestes says to Zeus: "I *am* my freedom. No sooner had you created me than I ceased to be yours . . . And there was nothing left in heaven, nor anyone to give me orders . . . But I must blaze my trail. For I, Zeus, am a man, and every man must find out his own way."

time. Kierkegaard tells the story of a ship's captain who has to decide just when his ship must come about. The vessel makes headway all the time. He has a few moments to make up his mind: "If he forgets to take account of the headway, there comes at last an instant when there no longer is any question of either/or, not because he has chosen but because he has neglected to choose, which is equivalent to saying, because others have chosen for him, because he has lost himself."

Most choices we make are admittedly trivial and inconsequential—choice of a necktie, choice of a restaurant, choice of a movie. A serious choice is a choice between actions involving fundamental values. It calls for deep concentration, a looking into oneself. However, I must not be content merely to apply an abstract moral principle. This is a weak choice, reliance on a rule rather than on myself. I should choose the course of action that seems uniquely right in this particular situation. I should seek not *the* way but *my* way.[6]

The hardest choices to make are often those between alternative goods. Two courses of action seem to have an equally good claim on us—which course do we take? Sartre tells the story of a young man who must decide whether to stay home and support his destitute mother or join the Free French. Kant's categorical imperative will not help him, nor will the Golden Rule. What must he do? He must act according to his strongest feeling. The young man reflects: "I ought to choose whatever pushes me in one direction. If I feel that I love my mother enough to sacrifice everything else for her—my desire for vengeance, for action, for adventure—then I'll stay with her." And so he did.

If I am an existentialist teacher, I urge the student to take

[6] I should point out that the existentialist does not reject moral principles as such, only abstract ones. Buber, writing on education for character, puts this well: "No responsible person remains a stranger to norms. But the command inherent in a genuine norm never becomes a maxim and the fulfillment of it never a habit. Any command that a great character takes to himself in the course of his development does not act in him as part of his consciousness or as material for building up his exercises but remains latent in a basic layer of his substance until it reveals itself to him in a concrete way." (*Between Man and Man*, op. cit., p. 114.)

responsibility for, and to deal with, the results of his actions. To act is to produce consequences. He must accept that these consequences are the issue of his choice, but at the same time he must not submit to them as unalterable, for this is to assume that freedom is exhausted in a single act. Freedom is never exhausted, and each consequence poses the need for further choice. I would teach him that his life is his own to lead and that no one else can lead it for him. It is pointless to blame his failures on environment, family, temperament, or the influence of others. These conditions are for choice to challenge. Whatever may have happened to the student in the past, the future is his to make.

Does this attitude lead to a ruthless disregard of others, to *my* fulfillment at the expense of yours? Not at all. True freedom implies not egoism but *communion*. The egoist is driven by a narrow self-interest. With him choice is not self-fulfillment but self-limitation. Freedom, open and dynamic, longs for other centers of freedom, other persons. It does not calculate but gives. The fulfillment of freedom is communion with others.

But we should not confuse this communion with mere familiarity. Communion is a certain intimacy with another person called by Buber "inclusion" and by Marcel "presence." You and I are in communion when we meet as independent selves to share a single experience. Each of us preserves his uniqueness.[7] I do not absorb you, nor do you me. Our communion is not an obliteration of selfhood in passion, but a dialogue in which I hear what passes in your mind and heart and you what passes in mine.[8] Listen to Buber: "The inner

[7] Nicholas Berdyaev, *Slavery and Freedom*, Scribners, New York, 1944, p. 42: "Egoistic self-containment and concentration upon the self, and the inability to issue forth from the self is original sin, which prevents the realization of the full life of the personality and hinders its strength from becoming effective. . . . Personality presupposes a going out from the self to another and to others. It lacks air and is suffocated when left shut up in itself."

[8] Cf. Maurice Merleau-Ponty, *Phenomenology of Perception*, Routledge & Kegan Paul, London, 1962, p. 334: "In the experience of dialogue there is constituted between the other person and myself a common ground; my thought and his are interwoven into a single fabric, my worlds and those

growth of the self is not accomplished, as people like to suppose today, in man's relation to himself, but . . . in the making present of another self and in the knowledge that one is made present by his own self to the other."[9]

Familiarity is not to be despised. It is natural and socially desirable. Nevertheless, it is incomplete, not a fulfillment of the self but a potential "waiting to be used." If as a teacher I assume the style and gestures for which convention calls, I may touch only the surfaces of my students' lives. I must go beyond familiarity and open myself to them. I must come to them unreservedly, creating the trust from which spring communion and true self-fulfillment.

According to the existentialist a moral act may be performed for itself or for an end. But a man must create his own ends. If he adopts the ends of a group or of society, he must make these ends his own by deciding in any situation that *this* is the end to aim at. The end is seized in the situation. It is not a standard to which acts conform but a goal at which an act is aimed. When moral principles are treated as external standards requiring certain sorts of behavior, they are turned into instruments of enslavement. Action becomes mere conduct and the individual submits to what is external to him.

As a teacher, then, I must not simply impose discipline. Rather, I must ask each student to accept the discipline that he sees as worthwhile in itself or as worthwhile for some end, such as his own intellectual development or the harmony of the class. It will be said by some that this is a counsel of perfection. Of course it is. It is an ideal to be striven for. Often I will fail to attain it, and so will my students. I may become a martinet; they may become anarchists. But we must try again. Neither repression nor anarchy is the answer. We must aim for the freedom and fulfillment of all, teacher and students together.

---

of my interlocutor are called forth by the state of the discussion, and they are inserted into a shared operation of which neither of us is the creator . . . we are collaborators for each other in consummate reciprocity. Our perspectives merge into each other, and we co-exist through a common world."

[9] Martin Buber, "Distance and Relation," *The Hibbert Journal*, **XLIX** (January 1951), 112 f.

KNOWING

Much existential thinking on the nature of knowledge is grounded in "phenomenology," a world view that seeks to describe the appearance of things and events *as they present themselves directly to our private consciousness.* These things and events thus possess a subjective as well as an objective reality. By "subjective reality" I refer to the immediate and personal relationships that all of us develop with nature and that children will seek to experience when they play hookey from school. Yes, the woods, the rocks, and the birds all have their own objective reality, and science tries to explain it. More importantly, however, we have our own understanding of reality, and in his essay, "On the Future of our Educational Institutions," Nietzsche advises us to heed the student's yearning for an intimate communion with nature on his own terms:

"The woods, the rocks the winds, the vulture, the flowers, the butterfly, the meads, the mountain slopes, must all speak to him in their own language; in them, he must, as it were, come to know himself again in countless reflections and images, in a variegated round of changing visions; and in this way he will unconsciously and gradually feel the metaphysical unity of all things in the great image of nature, and at the same time tranquilize his soul in the contemplation of her eternal endurance and necessity."

More recently, Merleau-Ponty, in his *Primacy of Perception* (Northwestern University, 1964), talks about a "grasping of external spaces through our own bodily situation (in which) a system of possible movements . . . radiates from us to our environment." Our bodies are not in space like things; they *inhabit* or *haunt* space; they represent our "expression to the world."

Thus, my knowledge depends on my understanding of reality, on my own interpretation of the nature of being. What, then, is "being"? In his *Philosophy of Existentialism* (Citadel, 1961), Marcel is quick to tell us that being is an "extremely difficult" concept to explain; in fact, Heidegger devoted his entire professional life to a systematic interpretation (without finishing the task). In Marcel's view, "being" is that mysterious something which remains after we have stripped reality of everything we think we have successfully described. Being, then, is not a definable substance, or category, or entity, but rather a "mystery" that each of us must encounter personally.

Now what is mysterious cannot be the same as what is unknown, for what is unknown may eventually become known, whereas what is mysterious by its very nature can never be known. Being-as-mystery is something that each one of us must understand for himself and make his private project. Merleau-Ponty says the same thing somewhat differently (*Sense and Non-Sense*, Northwestern University, 1964): "Reality begins . . . only when we cease to live in the evidence of the object . . . and perceive the radical subjectivity of all our experience as inseparable from truth." The test of being is always being-for-me.

If, then, we are to behave as existentialists, we must rethink our conception of knowledge. Subject matter, codified knowledge, should be treated neither as an end in itself nor as a means of preparing the student for an occupation or career. It should be used, rather, as a means toward self-development and self-fulfillment. Instead of subjecting the student to the matter, let the matter be subject to the student. Let the student "appropriate" to himself any knowledge he studies, that is, let him make it his own. In the process of learning, the person must be sovereign over the textbook.

School subjects, then, should become tools for the realization of the person, not impersonal disciplines to which all must submit alike. Let the growing person think out truths for himself, not Truth in the abstract but *his* truths. I do not mean by this that we should encourage him to believe whatever he likes. Rather, we should say to him, "These things have been found true by many people; now see for yourself whether they are true or not. If you do not find them true, say so, and let us discuss them together." For example, it is not enough for Newton's laws of motion to be true for scientists. The student must find them true for himself. He must be able to incorporate them within his view of the world.

This is what the pure specialist does not do. Specialization diminishes a man. The specialist is the creature of his knowledge, not the master of it. As Nietzsche pointed out, "A specialist in science begins to resemble nothing but a factory workman who spends his whole life in turning one particular screw or handle on a certain instrument or machine."[10] The school must see to it that the pupil who specializes continues to·advance in knowledge of the human condition. Specialized studies must go hand in hand with humane ones, and specialization must be humanized as much as possible. The man must be master of his specialty. On this Karl Jaspers has spoken clearly (*Man in the Modern Age*): "For his activities in every situation and in all occupations man needs a specific expert knowledge concerning things and concerning himself. But expert knowledge alone is never adequate for it only becomes significant in virtue of him who possesses it."

Education should also provide an insight into those experiences in which man is most aware of the human condition, experiences such as suffering, conflict, guilt, and death. These are always with us. Death may strike you or me at any time. Death places life in question; it confronts us with the contingency of our existence. Guilt is always with us. Where have we gone wrong? Are we now right? What is our responsibility to the black man? To the Japanese maimed at Hiroshima? To the millions shattered in Vietnam? To the people we have used, the pupils we have failed? We cannot escape suffering, conflict, guilt, and death. We must seek to understand them and meet them with wisdom.

[10] Friedrich Wilhelm Nietzsche, *On the Future of Our Educational Institutions*, Macmillan, New York, 1924, p. 39. Note that the existentialist does not condemn science as such, only the failure to educate scientists to be whole men as opposed to technicians. In *The Myth of Sisyphus* Camus puts the matter this way: "All the knowledge of this earth will give me nothing to assure me that this world is mine. You enumerate its laws and in my thirst for knowledge I admit that they are true. You take apart its mechanism and my hope increases. . . . But I realize that if through science I can seize phenomena and enumerate them, I cannot, for all that, comprehend the world."

TEACHING AND LEARNING

For one existentialist's conception of teaching and learning we turn to Martin Buber's theory of the "dialogue." A dialogue is a conversation between persons in which each person remains a subject for the other, a conversation, in Buber's terms, between an "I" and a "Thou."[11] The opposite of a dialogue is an act of verbal manipulation or dictation in which one person imposes himself on another, turning the latter into an object of his will expressed in speech. By Buber's standards most teaching is manipulation or dictation. The child is compelled to submit either to the will of the teacher directly or to a body of inflexible knowledge of which the teacher is custodian. Sometimes, of course, the tables may be turned and the teacher may become an object of the scorn or anger of his class.

Most of us are opposed to personal tyranny in the classroom, but Buber also opposed what he believed to be the tyranny of impersonal knowledge. Teaching, he said, could not be a true dialogue if the teacher were construed as an instructor, one who simply mediates between the pupil and the subject matter. When teaching is understood as instructing, the teacher is devalued into a means for the transfer of knowledge and the pupil is devalued into the product of this transfer. Knowledge is sovereign and persons become means and products. How, then, is knowledge to be transmitted? It is not to be transmitted at all but "offered." The teacher, said Buber, must familiarize himself fully with the subject he teaches, and take it into him-

---

[11] Although Buber's philosophy is highly personalistic, it is nevertheless a philosophy of human relations. In his view, true community could not come to pass until each individual accepted full responsibility for his neighbor. "Spirit is not in the *I* but between *I* and *Thou*. It is not like the blood that circulates in you but like the air in which you breathe." Social reality, then, is *mutuality*: "Through the Thou a man becomes I." But the I-Thou dialogue is not a mere verbal engagement. It is experiential, concrete, lodged in the "depth of living." See Martin Buber, *I and Thou*, Scribner's, New York, 1958, p. 64 especially. In *Between Man and Man*, op. cit., Buber writes (p. 88): "What teaches us the saying of *Thou* is not the instinct of origination but the instinct of communion."

self as the rich fruit of human activity. When the teacher has made the subject he teaches a part of his inner experience, he can present it to the pupil as something issuing from himself. Then teacher and pupil can meet as persons because the knowledge the teacher offers is no longer something extended to him but an aspect of his own condition.

When discussing a subject with his class, when teaching an aspect of literature or history, for example, the teacher seeks to introduce as many points of view as he can. He seeks to present the subject as a product of the thought of many men and as a focus of continuing thought. This indeed is the status of all knowledge that matters, for if knowledge is to endure, it must be reinterpreted and yield fresh significance in use. But it is not the teacher's intention to let the pupil choose whatever view of the subject he wishes. This would be irresponsible because the pupil is not an expert in the field. At the same time the teacher does not impose an interpretation or slip one past the pupil's guard, for this would devalue the student into an object of a teaching stratagem. Instead, after full discussion, the teacher offers the pupil what he believes to be the best view of the subject and asks him whether he will accept it.

The teacher presents the class with a variety of views to bring about a genuine discussion of the subject matter. The teacher has read widely and can set the subject before the class adequately. But he submits it for discussion. After discussion he offers the class the view that he himself has formed of the subject after long reflection. He asks each student to rest this view against his own experience, including the knowledge he has gathered in this class and in previous ones.

Suppose the student rejects the teacher's interpretation of the subject? Well, then, he rejects it. It is his right to do so. Existentialism insists not that the teacher be "successful" but that he be *honest*. Nevertheless, honesty leads to success, for if the teacher is honest with the pupil, he trusts him, and trust breeds its return. In an atmosphere of mutual trust the student knows that the teacher's interpretation of a subject is a wise one, and the teacher knows that the student will weigh this interpretation with the respect it deserves. Thus the dialogue that is education rests on trust between persons, a trust that the teacher must earn by integrity and create with skill.

What about subject matter? In the existentialist view no subject is more important (in itself) than any other. The subject that matters is the one in which the individual finds self-fulfillment and an awareness of the world. For some this subject is natural science; for many, it is history, literature, philosophy, or art. In these latter subjects the student becomes acquainted with the insights of great writers and thinkers into the nature of man in the world, into freedom, guilt, suffering, conflict, triumph, and death—themes that should engage the student intellectually and emotionally. The existentialist sees history, for example, in terms of man's struggle to realize his freedom. The student must commit himself to whatever period he is studying and immerse himself in its problems and personalities. The history he studies must fire his thoughts and feelings and become part of them.

When discussing the nature of human life, teachers should show that life is compounded of growth and decay, joy and tragedy. "Education for happiness" is a delusion. There is no happiness without pain, no ecstasy without suffering. Are the greatest achievements the work of happy men? Or of unsatisfied men striving for fulfillment? Education for security? For personal contentment? How illusory!

How does the existentialist teacher approach the subject of death? He suggests to his students that a knowledge of death increases one's awareness of life. If a student thinks hard about death, he becomes more conscious of the meaning of life. He ceases to drift; he is ready to sift the essential in his life from the trivial. That is why Blaise Pascal declared, "Live today as if you were to die tomorrow." The fact of death tells the student that he must make his life now.[12]

---

[12] In handling the topic of death the teacher could engage his students in debates or discussions on statements made by many thinkers throughout history. For example, the attitude of Judaism is expressed in Ecclesiastes: "There is a time to live and a time to die." When, indeed, *is* this time? Vespasian once declared, "An emperor should die standing up." What implication does this remark have for the practice of euthanasia? Marcus Aurelius

The teacher encourages the pupil to think for himself by engaging him in a dialogue. He questions the student about his ideas, proposes other ideas, and so leads him to choose between alternatives. The student sees then that truths do not happen to men, they are chosen by them. More than this, he becomes an actor in the drama of learning, not a spectator. He must work as hard as his teacher.

Unfortunately, too many students think that learning is just a matter of "soaking it up." They are wrong. Knowledge is acquired by active effort, by never closing the mind or heart, and by always seeking profounder truths than those one possesses. Some students keep this search to themselves. They do not open themselves to their teachers. However well they do in their work, they miss the opportunity for communion in the classroom. I always regret this. I believe that students and teachers should constantly interrogate one another.

The more I consider the troubled state of public education today, the more I am convinced that existentialists show the way to reform. Our children are herded into educational factories, where they are processed and fashioned alike regardless of their personal uniqueness. Our teachers are forced, or think they are forced, into teaching along lines laid down for them. This system alienates both pupil and teacher.[13] It is time to change it for a better one.

---

was a bit ruthless: "Thou hast embarked, thou hast made the voyage, thou art come to shore; now get out." Would suicide be an appropriate way to "get out"? The celebrated modern French author François Mauriac said recently that he was "fascinated" with the prospect of dying. He was in fact (at 80-odd years of age and sick in bed) eagerly awaiting his encounter with death. To what extent can we sympathize with such a view?

[13] Clark Moustakas eloquently expresses my point of view ("Alienation, Education, and Existential Life," Merrill Palmer Institute, Detroit, n.d., p. 16): "As it now stands the school is a powerful reinforcer of alienation in modern society. The teacher is alienated in himself; he does not exist as a real person in the classroom; he plays a part, a role; he fulfills duties and follows instructions. The teacher is alienated from his subject matter; it is external to his real world of feelings—anger, joy, sadness, loneliness, imagination, excitement, compassion—it is outside himself. The teacher is also alienated from the child; the child is perceived in categories and evaluative terms, as

Like Marcel, I believe that the school in its present form should be abolished. I would preserve a few of the facilities of the school—the library, the assembly hall, the gymnasium, the playing field—as facilities only. Young people could use these for studying and for group activities, such as games, play-acting, and musical performances. Instead of going to school for an education, the young person would go to a teacher. Student and teacher would meet in the teacher's home, or in the student's, or, if appropriate, on location. Sometimes the student would come alone, and sometimes with friends. I believe that under this arrangement the student would accomplish much more and in much shorter time than he does now. For the teacher would meet the student where he individually *is*.

I realize that this is a highly radical proposal and will be called impractical. But today's public schools are little more than a hundred years old, and when first conceived, were also called radical and impractical. I cannot help recalling the kind of school that J. D. Salinger's Teddy wanted. He would first "assemble" the students and "show them how to meditate." He would "try to show them how to find out who they *are*, not just what their names are and things like that. . . ." He would even try to "get them to empty out their heads" of all the stuff their parents and others had told them. If, as Camus said, "There is a whole civilization to be remade," Teddy's school would be an ideal way to start remaking it. Teachers alone cannot rebuild a civilization. But they can do much to educate individual pupils who may one day set about doing so.

---

slow or fast, as an outstanding achiever or an underachiever, as average or retarded, and in many, many other traits and classifications, all of which have relevance in the object relationship but not in encounter and in self-actualization. In such a setting, where the teacher is alienated from himself, from the subject matter and from his pupils, gradually but definitely, the teacher becomes an object among objects, a thing among things."

References

There are many articles on the meaning of existentialism for education but only two full-length books: my own *Existentialism and Education* (Wiley, 1965, 170 pp.), originally published in 1958; and Van Cleve Morris, *Existentialism in Education* (Harper and Row, 1966, 163 pp.). The only anthology I know, and one that has helped me in writing this essay, is Maxine Greene, Ed., *Existential Encounters for Teachers* (Random House, 1967, 174 pp.). The selections are from original writings by authors with existentialist views, and Greene's commentary is perceptive. There are many general studies of existentialism as such. My students particularly like William Barrett's *What Is Existentialism?* (Grove, 1965). *Existentialism from Dostoievsky to Sartre*, edited by Walter A. Kaufmann (Meridian Books, World Publishing Co., Cleveland and New York, 1956) is an excellent anthology. For ambitious students with a good background in formal philosophy I recommend George A. Schrader, Ed., *Existential Philosophers: Kierkegaard to Merleau-Ponty* (McGraw-Hill, 1967, 437 pp.).

5

Logic and Analysis

LOGIC AND PSYCHOLOGY

I have often wondered why teachers in training are usually taught so much psychology and so little logic. One explanation is that psychology, the study of individual behavior, tells teachers important things about how their students are likely to behave. Another explanation is that, whereas psychologists always have been interested in education, logicians, at any rate since the Middle Ages, have generally ignored it. There is also a third explanation. Psychology studies the *process* of thinking as it actually occurs. Formal logic, on the other hand, considers the *forms* taken by the ideas or arguments that thought produces. As a result, formal logic has seemed less applicable to the problems of teachers at work. Nevertheless, any notion that logic has little or nothing to say to the teacher in the classroom is profoundly mistaken. This chapter will, I hope, show that the study of logic and of the logical use of language has much to contribute to both the theory and the practice of education.

Whereas psychology studies the actual process of thinking, formal logic supplies rational forms for ordering the results of thought. Formal logic considers what sorts of arguments are valid. How any person actually thinks in order to produce these arguments is irrelevant to the logical validity of the arguments themselves. Admittedly, if a person is to produce logical arguments, he must be motivated to do so. But whether or not he produces them by intuition or slow calculation does not matter from a formal logical point of view. What matters is that he should wish to reach conclusions that are valid and should know when he does so. To implant the wish and to cultivate the knowledge are tasks of teaching.

At first a teacher may reward a student for thinking logically, that is, for drawing valid conclusions, and the student may for a while think logically in order to receive the reward. Gradually, however, if he is properly taught, the student may find such thought satisfying not only because it is rewarded but also because it is intellectually fruitful. He will find that one valid conclusion begets another, whereas inconsistency leads nowhere. Thus the *habit* of thinking logically can be cultivated by psychological means, that is, by specific tactics of teaching based on an understanding of human behavior.

Indeed, a knowledge of and a training in logic can in themselves affect a person's behavior. Other things being equal, a person who has studied logic will tend to be more rational and more intellectually aware than one who has not. He will be more likely to question his own prejudices and rationalizations. He will be less influenced by the specious pleading of others and more competent in spotting fallacies and inconsistencies in their arguments.

In education the question is often asked: Is it better to introduce content on the basis of an order present in the subject matter itself or according to the stage of development reached by the learner? Should the study of physics, for example, always follow that of algebra (logical order), or should these subjects be taught any time the learner is ready for them (psychological order)?

The logical presentation of subject matter is based on the theory that logical order already is built into it. Such order is a part of nature, we hear, or is assumed to be. Algebra, for example, has many components and we must know certain ones before we can understand others. We can also grasp certain operations in physics only after we know algebra.

Those who hold this theory are confident that if a student masters knowledge in this fashion, he will automatically think logically. The more extreme among them reject virtually all psychological considerations that interfere with this approach. They maintain that one of the chief purposes of learning subject matter is to give order to a mind that comes to it in a state of disorder. It is folly, they say, to allow an unordered, untrained mind to dictate what the order of subject matter should be or how it should be learned.

Psychological order, on the other hand, relates subject matter to the aims, interests, and experiences of the student. The learning process, astutely manipulated by the teacher, is initiated by the learner; his interest is aroused; his reflective powers are challenged; and his curiosity is gratified. The student and the subject matter "interact."

That logical and psychological order should not conflict but should go hand in hand is a proposition supported by most observers.[1] John Dewey identified the "psychological and logical" with "process and product" respectively. The psychological process, he said, becomes the means of understanding subject matter in its logical form. For the learner, the latter is an ideal to be achieved and not a starting point from which to proceed.[2] The learning process is "the progressive development of what is already experienced into a fuller and richer and

---

[1] John Dewey, *How We Think,* Heath, Boston, Mass., 1933, p. 84: "[They] are connected as the earlier and the terminal stages of the same process of learning."

[2] John Dewey, *Democracy and Education,* Macmillan, New York, 1916, p. 257.

more organized form, a form that gradually approximates the subject matter presented to the skilled, mature person."[3]

THE LOGIC OF INQUIRY

"Logic," said the iconoclastic English pragmatist F. S. C. Schiller, "is so much technical trivia . . . fit only to confuse students in examinations and inappropriate for a world of chance and change. We have no proof," he continued, "that the universe is logically organized. It may or may not be. In order to find out, we must experiment with the world, 'try it out', as it were."

Schiller was, of course, condemning only *formal* logic. But his remarks pave the way for us to seek answers through what has been called the "logic of inquiry," formulated by John Dewey. The subject of the logic of inquiry is the *process of inferring*. Where formal logic deals with the forms of arguments, the logic of inquiry seeks to establish the principles that men *ought* to observe in order to reach valid conclusions. Thus the logic of inquiry is prescriptive in that it recommends principles for men to follow. But it is also descriptive, since these, in Dewey's view, are the principles that men do in fact follow when they inquire successfully.

To inquire, said Dewey, is to resolve a problematic situation. This takes six steps, which will now be described in a school setting.[4]

---

[3] John Dewey, *Experience and Education*, Macmillan, New York, 1951, p. 87. Dewey's "activity principle" springs from the concepts just outlined, according to which students should learn actively. They must become consciously involved when a lecture is being presented and not just sit and take notes. They must "activate" their intelligence; in other words, they must prepare themselves psychologically to deal with subject matter in all its essentially logical nature.

[4] Dewey defined inquiry as "the controlled or directed transformation of an indeterminate situation into one that is so determinate in its constituent distinctions and relations as to convert the elements of the original situation into a unified whole." All logical forms, he said, "arise within the operations of inquiry and are concerned with control over inquiry so that it may yield

1. In the Deweyan view all thinking is a response to some difficulty that cannot be surmounted by instinct or routine. The student encounters such difficulties all the time, for he is always learning something new. Suppose, then, that I am a student in high school studying the events leading to World War II. I learn about the Versailles Treaty, the Depression, the inaction of the League of Nations, the Munich Agreement, and so forth. Still, I am dissatisfied. I have many supposed facts before me—the fact, for instance, that the Versailles Treaty imposed crippling reparations on Germany, and the fact that France and Britain acquiesced in the German occupation of Czechoslovakia. But these facts are not yet organized in a way that makes sense to me. They are "inert." They do not explain anything.

2. After a while I cease to be merely dissatisfied. I realize that the matter I am learning needs somehow to be given significance. Now, if I have been taught to think logically, I do not dismiss my dissatisfaction, but put it in the form of a problem or a question to be resolved. Why did World War II happen?

3. Having formulated the problem, I must find information to solve it. True, I already have learned much in class. But the very act of defining the problem suggests other areas to be explored; in this case, the events leading to the outbreak of war and the conditions that made those events possible, such as rearmament, mass unemployment, and the rise of totalitarian ideologies. The information I gather suggests possible solutions to the problem. For example, in considering the ideology of National Socialism, I encounter the concept of *Lebensraum* ("living space") and the principle that Germany must defend Western Europe against Asiatic invaders. These ideas may suggest that Germany went to war in order to forestall a threatened assault on Europe by the Soviet Union. Still, this is only one of a number of possibilities that I consider.

warranted assertions." John Dewey, *Logic: The Theory of Inquiry*, Holt, New York, 1938, pp. 3-4, 104.

4. My next step is to evaluate these possibilities to see how consistent each is with the facts at my disposal and with the other hypotheses that have occurred to me. Clearly, I will find a number of causes of World War II, some of which will be more important than others. Hence I will consider each hypothesis in relation not only to the facts it covers but also to the other explanations with which it will cohere. In the process a number of hypotheses will be rejected—the hypothesis, for example, that Germany declared war in 1939 because a severe depression earlier had led to the formation of an authoritarian and warlike regime. This hypothesis breaks down because it fails to account for the fact that Britain, France, and the United States all suffered from a depression and yet became pacifist or isolationist rather than belligerent. A more likely hypothesis might be that Hitler only intended to attack Russia and that he found himself at war with the Western powers as a result of diplomatic misunderstandings. Another hypothesis might be that the failure of the Western powers to act at the time of Hitler's movements into Austria and Czechoslovakia encouraged the National Socialists to embark on a plan of world conquest.

5. I then test the more promising hypotheses experimentally by deducing their probable consequences and verifying whether these consequences hold good. Suppose I consider the hypothesis that World War II was caused by Hitler's desire to make Europe an Aryan fortress. First, I deduce the likely outcomes of this hypothesis: that Hitler would cooperate for a time with other Aryan peoples in Europe, that he would make all non-Aryan populations servants of the master race, and so forth. Then I check whether these consequences in fact took place. I investigate whether Hitler offered to cooperate with other Aryan nations, whether he in fact turned Slavic countries into vassal states, and so on.

6. Finally, I coordinate the hypotheses that I have verified objectively. They now constitute "warranted assertions," meaning that they are justified on the basis of the information I have examined and the range of hypotheses I have proposed to explain it. All such assertions, however, are tentative, since further information, broader or more penetrating hypotheses, or simply finer thinking, might invalidate them wholly or in part. Thus the knowledge I have acquired is provisional. But it is a basis for further inquiry, because it offers a means for exploring the same ground more thoroughly and because it provides a vantage point for much broader generalizations, as, for example, about the causes of all wars.[5]

What are the special characteristics of this kind of thinking? First, it is *scientific*. It leads me to define a problem, gather information, propose hypotheses, predict their consequences, verify the latter experimentally, and coordinate the findings. Second, it is *critical*. It makes me consider alternative possibilities, examine as many facts as I can, delay judgment until the facts have been verified, and verify ideas with reference to facts rather than personal preferences. It makes me unwilling to take things for granted and leads me to consider all knowledge as tentative and open to revision. Finally, it is *reflective*. It stops me from jumping to conclusions. Instead of doing the first thing that enters my head, I pause to consider whether there are better alternatives.

Many problems within individual disciplines lend themselves

---

[5] Recently, the factor of *relevance* has taken on greater significance for the logic of inquiry. See Joseph J. Schwab, "The Structure of the Natural Sciences," in G. W. Ford and Lawrence Pugno, Eds., *The Structure of Knowledge and the Curriculum*, Rand McNally, Chicago, 1964, pp. 38-39, where Schwab summarizes his criticisms and gives implications for a "revised version of the schoolbook study of the short-term syntax of the sciences." Existing versions, he says (p. 37), omit a step preceding step one, which "refers to the discrimination of relevant data but fails to tell us in what way relevance and irrelevance are determined." Relevance, in other words, must have a reference. Schwab then outlines his own version: "(1) The formulation of a problem (from juxtaposing a principle of inquiry—a substantive structure—and index phenomena); (2) the search for data that will suggest possible solutions to this problem; (3) reformulation of the problem to include these possible solutions; (4) a determination of the data necessary to solve the problem; (5) a plan of experiment that will elicit the data required; (6) execution of the experiment and accumulation of the desired data; (7) interpretation of the data by means of the guiding substantive structures together with previous knowledge possessed by the investigator."

to this kind of thinking—the sociological problem, for instance, of population mobility and its probable effect on the education of youth. Clearly, a question as complicated as this should not be attempted without several years' study of sociology together with some knowledge of other social sciences. But there are simpler sociological problems to which the method can be applied at an earlier age. In other words, once the pupil has been introduced to some area of study, he can use the problem-solving method not only to handle what he knows but also to explore further.

The problem-solving method may be applied to issues in contemporary life, such as civil rights, taxation, and Federal aid to schools. These are "molar" problems, so called because they cut across a range of disciplines. Problems of taxation, for example, call for a knowledge of law, finance, economics, and accounting. Problems of Federal aid to education require a knowledge of history, political science, sociology, and economics. One of the main tasks in dealing with such problems is to judge what knowledge and what disciplines are relevant to them, an art that can be learned only by actually handling problems that involve a number of disciplines.

Educators might help here by offering a problems course in such topics as juvenile delinquency, disarmament, and central-city decay. The primary purpose of such a course would be to nurture an intelligent and flexible cast of mind rather than to provide knowledge or ready-made solutions.[6] In particular, it would help cultivate the ability to think logically, interpret a problem through different intellectual frames (sociological, ethical, and so forth), and decide matters in concert with others. To be effective, the course would probe only a few problems in depth. The pupils would engage in such operations

[6] Cf. Harry S. Broudy, B. Othanel Smith, and Joe R. Burnett, *Democracy and Excellence in American Secondary Education: A Study in Curriculum Theory*, Rand McNally, Chicago, 1964, pp. 241-243. A problems course may also be instituted to coordinate the different disciplines and accompany the general education program throughout the junior and senior high school. See also Arno A. Bellack, "Knowledge Structure and the Curriculum," in Stanley Elam, Ed., *Education and the Structure of Knowledge*, Fifth Annual Phi Delta Kappa Symposium on Educational Research, Rand McNally, Chicago, 1964, pp. 275-276.

as defining the problem to be solved, tracing its implications, gathering relevant facts and theories, examining the causes of disagreement, proposing alternative solutions, and evaluating them.[7]

LOGIC IN TEACHING

Logic may also be applied to the *act of teaching*, where teaching is understood to be a special way of making things known to others. Here teaching may be considered a system of actions varied in form and content but directed toward learning. It is in the performance of these actions and in the interactions of the teacher with his students that learning takes place. These actions and interactions are of course personal. But they are also logical, in that they have a certain structure, a certain order, such that no matter where in the world teaching takes place, it does so in accordance with operations that reflect the very nature of a teaching-learning situation.

What are these logical operations? How may they be analyzed?[8] The act of teaching may be said to involve three variables: (1) the teacher's behavior, which is the independent variable, (2) the pupil's behavior, which is the dependent variable, and (3) various postulated entities, such as memories,

---

[7] The utility of the logic of inquiry is still disputed. Critics maintain that in practice it is less effective than the techniques of problem solving formulated within the disciplines themselves. It also tends, they say, to constrict the inquiring mind. My own reply would be that it is *adaptable* (if not immediately applicable) to any subject matter at almost any level. And *any* formulation of a way of thinking by its very nature can be accused of constricting the mind. But the argument is too lengthy to pursue here. For a philosophic analysis of Dewey's theory of inquiry and resultant debates see Robert R. Wellman, "Dewey's Theory of Inquiry: The Impossibility of Its Statement," *Educational Theory*, **XIV**, 2 (April 1964), 103 ff., answered by Philip Eddy, "On the Statability of Dewey's Theory of Inquiry," *Educational Theory*, **XV**, 4 (October 1965), 321 ff., and rebutted by Wellman, op. cit., 327 ff.

[8] For a complete account, see the works of B. Othanel Smith (and others) cited in the References at the end of this chapter. For an earlier brief statement, see B. Othanel Smith, "A Concept of Teaching," in B. Othanel Smith and Robert H. Ennis, Eds., *Language and Concepts in Education*, Rand McNally, Chicago, 1961, pp. 86-101.

beliefs, needs, and inferences, which are intervening variables.[9]

In the course of teaching, these variables—the teacher's acts, the pupil's acts, and the postulated entities—are related in many ways. The teacher's acts are followed by various postulated states in the pupil which cause him to behave in certain ways. The teacher cannot observe these states directly; he cannot personally witness interests, needs, motives, and the like; but he can, and often does, *infer* them from the pupil's overt behavior. For example, he may infer from the pupil's reactions that he is interested in what he is doing or that he would prefer to do something else. The pupil's actions in turn lead to various postulated states in the teacher, which then give rise to actions. The cycle begins again, as the teacher's behavior produces postulated states in the pupil, and so on. The process of teaching continues in this fashion until the teacher concludes either that the pupil has learned what he intended him to learn or that there is nothing to be gained from teaching him any more at the moment.

Independent variables in the teacher's behavior consist of "verbal," "performative," and "expressive" acts. *Verbal acts* are of three kinds: (1) logical operations, such as defining, classifying, explaining, and the like; (2) directive operations instructing the pupil in what he is to do, such as write on a blackboard, read a poem, or recite a multiplication table; and (3) admonitory operations, such as praising, blaming, reassuring, and so on. *Performative acts* are of the motor variety but may be accompanied by words. The teacher shows the pupil how to do something, such as regulate a Bunsen burner. *Expressive acts* reveal the psychological state of the teacher, exemplified in facial expression, tone of voice, body movements, and so forth.

The dependent variables can be similarly classified. The learner performs many verbal actions. Some of them are logical operations, and their purpose is to indicate that the pupil

[9] It should be pointed out that the expression "intervening variable" has been used in so many different ways that psychologists as a whole now tend to avoid it. (It has always struck me as rather like "phlogiston" or Hull's "black box"—a place to put vague concepts that refer, as John Locke said of "substance," to "I know not what.")

understands what he is being taught. He rarely performs verbal actions that are directive or admonitory, since telling-how-to and praising or blaming are typically the teacher's responsibility. When the pupil behaves performatively (taking part in athletics, for example, or setting up laboratory equipment), he normally does so to practice the actions themselves rather than to instruct anyone. The pupil also behaves expressively. He smiles or frowns, slumps or sits erect, speaks firmly or uncertainly, and so on. Such behavior, though rarely addressed to anyone, indicates to the teacher how the pupil is feeling.

Admittedly, "logic" used in this sense is not the rigorous enterprise normally understood when we use the word, but it does involve such elements as structure, propriety, and rationality when dealing with events like teaching. Thus, when we construe teaching as a system of actions intended to induce learning, and analyze the model of the teaching process based on it, we emerge with an objective approach to the study of teaching. Where previously research into the effectiveness of teaching methods has proceeded from definitions of teaching that reflects a preference for one method or another, the findings being inconclusive, we now see the actions of the teacher as they really are, relatively undistorted by our preconceptions. Thus we are, or should be, able to assess more accurately the strengths and weaknesses of different teaching methods.[10]

ANALYSIS AND LANGUAGE

In the chapter on the Relevance of Philosophy I outlined three modes of philosophy, of which *analysis* was one. The hallmarks of philosophic analysis are a concern with logic and

---

[10] The application of logic to the act of teaching is far from being as definitive as we would like, for teaching, being a human endeavor, resists our most earnest attempts to establish a structure for it. Also, the success of construing teaching as an act involving logical operations depends chiefly on the expertise of the teacher and the kind of subject matter he imparts. (Here I do not refer to method or purpose, but simply to a practical knowledge of what actually happens or comes close to happening when any teacher teaches.)

a concern with language. Analysis turns away from speculation and prescription. It refuses to offer theories of the universe or rules for the good life. Its goal is to clarify thoughts. This goal has been aptly described by Ludwig Wittgenstein:

"The object of philosophy is the logical clarification of thoughts.

"Philosophy is not a theory but an activity.

"A philosophical work consists essentially of quotations.

"The result of philosophy is not a number of 'philosophical propositions,' but to make propositions clear.

"Philosophy should make clear and delimit sharply the thoughts which otherwise are, as it were, opaque and blurred."[11]

A concern with clear, logical thinking implies an equal concern with the language in which thoughts are expressed. It is pointless to look *through* language at thoughts or propositions if that language is opaque and blurred. One must also look *at* language.

In the combination of logical and linguistic analysis—analysis of the logic of arguments through analysis of the language in which they are expressed—philosophers of this persuasion believe that they have found a means of resolving most of the traditional problems of philosophy. Such problems, they say, are confusions in thought arising at least in part from confusion in language. Misleading constructions, obscure idioms, and ambiguous phrases generate philosophers' perplexities. These problems must be dissolved by investigating the logical implications of the sentences in which they occur. Among the leading exponents of this view are G. E. Moore, Ludwig Wittgenstein, Gilbert Ryle, Peter F. Strawson, and John L. Austin.

The analyst maintains that philosophic problems arise in the course of our attempts to order and explain known facts. These problems cannot be solved by an appeal to the facts

[11] Ludwig Wittgenstein, *Tractatus Logico-Philosophicus*, Humanities Press, New York, 1955, p. 77 (4.112).

themselves, because the point of issue is how the facts are to be described. The problems are created by the complexities of language. Since a given word or expression normally has a range of uses, it is easy to confuse these uses and to employ one where another is appropriate. For example, the word "growth" is used in a number of contexts from biology to education. If we transfer the biological sense of growth to the context of education, we unwittingly tangle two sets of logical implications, those of growth in biology and those of growth in education. To compare the growth of a child with that of a plant is misleading, because the word "growth" implies different things in these different contexts.

The role of analysis, then, is essentially therapeutic: to clear the mind by revealing the sources of conceptual perplexity. Analysis does not "solve" problems, it "dissolves" them. Analysis examines the customary uses of the expressions and types of expression that are involved in the problems of philosophy, and it seeks to indicate where philosophers have overextended or misapplied such expressions to produce paradox or perplexity. The standard of correct use is normally actual speech, or the ways in which words are customarily used in various contexts. Actual speech is the most reliable guide to meaning, for it must meet what for the analyst is the most stringent of all tests of effective communication, that of constant use.[12]

Analysis has answered readily to the study of education. As a discipline or branch of knowledge, education is highly practical, in the sense that the process it studies (that of being educated) is a normal experience in the life of every person. What is true of the study of education as a whole is true of its

[12] P. F. Strawson, "Construction and Analysis," in *The Revolution in Philosophy*, Gilbert Ryle, introd., Macmillan, London, 1956, p. 103. Cf. also J. L. Austin, "A Plea for Excuses," *Proceedings of the Aristotelian Society*, **LVIII** 8 (1956-57): ". . . our common stock of words embodies all the distinctions men have found worth drawing, and the connections they have found worth making . . . these surely are likely to be more numerous, more sound, since they have stood up to the long test of the survival of the fittest, and more subtle, at least in all ordinary and reasonably practical matters, than any that you or I are likely to think up in our armchairs. . . ."

philosophy. The problems and the language of educational philosophy are for the most part those of general life. At the same time some fundamental concepts that occur in educational discourse also appear in a number of realms of inquiry, such as psychology, sociology, and economics. They include "knowing," "learning," "socializing," "valuing," and "ascertaining." When analyzing these concepts, the educator must examine their meanings in many different contexts. Then he will be able to spot the ambiguities that are caused when meanings appropriate to certain contexts are imported into others. Education also possesses concepts of its own, such as "subject matter," "mastery," "readiness," and "character training." These are not only topics of theoretical debate but also fiercely defended justifications of many practical school policies, a fact that adds to the difficulty of analyzing them.

Thus the study of education draws heavily on ideas in general currency as well as on the ideas of a range of related disciplines. As a result, not a few educational concepts carry a number of logical implications corresponding to the different spheres in which these concepts are used; in consequence, they are highly ambiguous. One of these concepts is that of "adjustment," which is used, among other places, in psychology and in education.[13] Another is that of "need." When a school says that it exists "to meet the needs of students," what is it really saying? That it has assessed *all* the needs of its students and can meet them? Or just *some* of the needs? If so, which ones? Perhaps "needs" could be dissolved into a statement about the aims of education as seen and practiced by School X. Or perhaps the word means nothing at all. Or take "adjustment." To which part of the school is Johnny supposed to adjust—the routine, the teacher, the curriculum, the athletic program, or what? Does he become less free by adjusting or

[13] For an analysis of this concept, see C. J. B. Macmillan, "The Concept of Adjustment," in George F. Kneller, Ed., *Introduction to the Philosophy of Education*, Wiley, New York, 1964, pp. 82 ff. See also B. Paul Komisar, " 'Need' and the 'Needs-Curriculum'," in B. Othanel Smith and Robert H. Ennis, Eds., *Language and Concepts in Education*, Rand McNally, Chicago, Ill., 1961, pp. 24-42.

more free? Does anybody—in fact, can anybody—adjust to an *entire* school? Even if a student could adjust to the school, is it not better for the school to adjust to the student?

The word "relevant," too, has become a fashionable term for judging the success or failure of schooling. But the term lends itself to almost as many meanings as there are people who use it. "Relevance" can be used to convey an emphasis on vocational studies, on a problems approach to learning, on learning for its own sake, on a theoretical analysis of the human condition, or on whatever the speaker regards as the end of a good education. Perhaps most often it is used to indicate that the school has an obligation to serve a particular community, or a special subculture, or a certain class of people. An education that is relevant, we hear, is one that goes out into the streets, into factories, homes, organizations, and settlements. It takes place in communes and collectives. It is geared to individual and racial hopes, aspirations, and special interests. It even serves or should serve to overthrow a "sick" society and to revolutionize the value system of our culture. Thus the slogan, "Education should be relevant to the needs of the community," can mean anything and everything. For what is meant by "education"? What precisely are the "needs" that education is physically and spiritually capable of meeting? And what is a "community"? Is it a place, a feeling, a condition, a unified set of purposes, an autonomous, self-subsistent society, or what?

Nevertheless, analysis is no substitute for factual knowledge. If we dispute how far education should "meet the needs" of the pupil, we must know what these needs are at different ages and whether they vary by region, by social class, by economic status, and so on. This knowledge can come only from factual inquiry. Nor can analysis provide us with the moral beliefs that are necessary for decisions about educational practice. For instance, the problem of adjustment is to a large extent a moral one. Analysis cannot provide us with the moral principles that we need to decide it. But it can make us aware of the assumptions and implications that these principles involve. It can clarify the concepts, slogans, exhortations, and the like that are put forward in arguments on "neutrality," "commitment," and so forth.

So far I have described what analysis is. Now I will do some analysis myself. I have chosen two concepts to analyze: "teaching" and "equality." My treatment must be short and simple to fit into this chapter. But perhaps enough can be said to challenge the reader to study these concepts further.

CONCEPT OF TEACHING

Classic definitions state that teaching is "imparting knowledge," "training in a skill," "giving instruction." But they tell us very little about what imparting knowledge amounts to, what goes into the task of training in a skill, or what happens when one gives instruction. In fact, if we look up "impart," we find that one of its meanings is "teach." Under "instruct" the first synonym is also "teach." We are a little better off with the word "train," which dictionaries associate with "strong teaching." To train is to "subject to instruction" with the idea of producing "efficient performance." Still, we can have weak training, the kind that does not result in efficient performance. The dictionary, then, does not help us to distinguish among all the synonyms of teaching. In fact, it leads us round and round and back where we started. Let us therefore move out of the pages of the dictionary and into the more enlightening realm of analysis.

First of all, what does a teacher do when he teaches? Does he just talk, or tell, or relate, or what? Actually, he does all these things, but *with a purpose*. And that purpose is to get students to learn. Teaching, then, is an "intentional activity," one that aims to bring about learning. The teacher describes, explains, questions, and evaluates; he urges, threatens, and cajoles; in short, he does many things to get students to learn the sorts of things he thinks they should learn and in a manner of which he approves. Parents and others do this too, but with a difference. Teachers are more "professional," meaning that they know a great deal about (a) what they teach, (b) how to teach it, and (c) whom they are teaching. A teacher's primary task is to get students to know or to do things in a formal way. This means that he structures knowledge or skills in such a way as to cause the student not only to learn them but also to remember them and do something with them. The teacher also evaluates the student; hence, the student is challenged to learn and to remember because he knows that in one way or another he will be examined. In short, unlike other people, the teacher engages in what has been called "didactic," as distinct from "ordinary," discourse. That is, he avoids casual, unstudied conversation in favor of deliberate, weighed communication. He designs his teaching in such a way that the student will think hard about and remember what he is learning.

Now of course, all discourse is intended to influence people in some way. A question is meant to elicit a reply, a threat to deter, a condolence to comfort, and a promise to reassure. The purpose of didactic discourse is not merely to enable the student to repeat what he has been taught but also to say and do a number of things with it. When a teacher explains the use of the relative pronoun, his prime aim is not that the pupil should repeat this explanation (although no doubt he intends this too) but that the pupil should use the relative pronoun correctly. When he sets forth the causes of the French Revolution, he intends that the pupil should be able not only to repeat this knowledge in an examination but also, and more importantly, to use it in assessing other prerevolutionary situations past and present, in short, to apply the knowledge he has received.[14]

Not all teaching is didactic discourse. We can teach by demonstration, by drill, by example, and by any method that results in the kind of learning we want to achieve. In essence, however, the language of teaching is didactic discourse. There are several advantages in accepting this view. For one thing, the

---

[14] Didactic discourse can also be internal. A person can teach himself to say and do things that differ from the style in which the teaching was given. For example, having taught himself elementary logic, he can then detect flaws in other people's reasoning. In fact, people often learn more through self-instruction than from a human teacher.

content of didactic discourse is largely independent of the deliverer, the recipient, and the occasion of the delivery. Other things being equal, the information involved can be delivered by any appropriate qualified person to any properly prepared learner on any suitable occasion. Thus if a student misses a lesson, he can make it up later. For another, the content can be preserved, compared, criticized, and added to, so that what is taught to one generation can be imparted to another generation years later, whereas mere talking, telling, and narrating are more greatly conditioned by who talks and when and where.[15]

But, you will ask, where does learning come in? Teaching, I have said, is an effort to bring about learning. The converse, however, is not true. Efforts to achieve learning do not necessarily require a human teacher. Furthermore, although the achievement of learning is the hallmark of successful teaching, it is not sufficient in itself to determine *good* teaching. All depends on the appropriateness of the learning achieved. I might be able to teach Johnny the multiplication table, and then when he shows me that he has learned (and remembers) it, I can say I have taught him successfully. But I may not have taught him as well as I could all the things he should know about the concept of multiplication. I may not have allowed him to make discoveries on his own. I may have looked for quick results when I should have spent more time building sounder knowledge. So teaching now appears to involve "goodness" as well as "success."

What are some of the conditions of good teaching? The first is *continuity*. We do not teach a single lesson and let it go

---

[15] Didactic discourse also helps us to distinguish between kinds of human communication. It involves intellectual operations that, in the opinion of most educators, are "higher" than other kinds of behavior and indeed should govern them. In most civilized nations intellectual work is "highly" favored. It is the work of those who, like the readers of this essay, have received a "higher" education and can give it to others. If intellectual power as generated through didactic discourse ceases to be favored by a culture, that culture will atrophy. Cf. Gilbert Ryle, "The Intellect," in Israel Scheffler, Ed., *Philosophy and Education*, Allyn and Bacon, Boston, 1958, pp. 133-140.

at that. We teach lessons both cumulatively and in order of difficulty. We take into consideration the age, aptitude, and ability of the educand, and we organize our activities over a relatively long span of time. This is quite different from the way nonteachers behave. Parents inform their children about many things, such as religion, morals, and sex. But under the conditions we have given for the application of the concept "teaching," parents do not usually teach. Indeed, this is one reason why, in the opinion of many, information on morals and sex should be taught in school. Here, in theory, if not necessarily in practice, morality and sex may be learned as a consequence of good teaching. The second condition of good teaching is the *intentional practicalization* of what is taught (and learned). Telling, informing, and relating do not *require* learning—not even good telling, informing, and relating. But good teaching does, and teaching is good only when the pupil uses and lives out what he has learned freely and responsibly.

Good teaching involves yet a third condition, *concept formation*. The good teacher ensures that learners acquire patterns of thought and action that will not only endure but will also render specific commands superfluous. There is a vast difference between people who (a) have been told to be honest, (b) have learned to be honest, and (c) have learned that they *ought* to be honest. I can tell Johnny to be honest (a command); but if I teach him well, he will learn (a) what honesty is, (b) why it is a good thing, and (c) why he *ought* to be honest. I would also expect him actually to *be* honest, because he has come to *believe* (as well as know) that he *should* be honest. The challenge then for the teacher is not only to inform students about honesty (or anything else, for that matter) but also to try to get them to be honest from their own convictions critically arrived at.

Now of course, it is possible to teach well only to have the student quite responsibly reject (a) the teacher, (b) the knowledge, and (c) the way the knowledge is presented. This is a risk all teachers must take. Indeed, having taken the risk, having encouraged critical reflection, impartial scrutiny, and the taking of positions, we find ourselves confronted today with rebellious students everywhere. But unless the rebels can be shown to be irresponsible and unreasonable, we must happily conclude that some teachers have done their job well—very well indeed. "Progress," we hear, "is the result of discontented minds."

In a nutshell, when we say certain conditions are necessary for good teaching, we mean that students are taught the habits and norms of critical thought and behavior. We do not simply teach students how to be good citizens, as if citizenship were a set of skills, but also *to be* good citizens (or give good cause for being otherwise). We teach them not merely what voting is but also how to vote and what voting is worth as a norm in political life.

Does good teaching include indoctrination? Yes, for a good teacher cannot help indoctrinating. He will tell his class what he thinks is good and bad in our culture, but he will also praise the good and condemn the bad. Since education, as I have said, is essentially a normative affair, a teacher will always reveal his values. He will teach what he thinks students ought to learn (as well as what he is directed to teach).

Indoctrination, then, is not in itself contrary to good teaching. Rather, *it is the content of what is indoctrinated that matters, together with the method used.* Some people think that indoctrination in democracy is a contradiction in terms (since democracy implies freedom of teaching and learning). It is not. "The qualifications for self-government," said Thomas Jefferson, "are not innate. They are the result of habit and long training." Democracy rests on certain established principles, and we have every reason to teach for the acceptance of these principles, in short, to inculcate a belief in them. This does not mean that we cannot criticize them. It means that the teacher has every right to use his influence on his students when he is teaching about our political system. He is privileged and, some think, duty-bound to communicate the ideals of the culture, among which is included the right to criticize the culture. To the demurrer that teachers should remain "neutral," I can only reply that this too is taking a position, although not a very effective one. The neutral teacher quickly loses his appeal, for education is not a neutral but a value-laden enterprise.[16]

It should now be clear that teaching is also a method of inducing acceptable belief. But we must show how teaching differs from other methods of inducing belief, such as debating, threatening, forcing, propagandizing, bribing, and so forth. Teaching differs from these primarily because it involves rationality, judgment, critical dialogue, and defensibility. Teaching induces belief through the exercise of free, rational judgment by the student. The teacher too gives reasons for the beliefs he wants to transmit, thus submitting his own judgments to the critical assessment of his students. The teacher then actually risks his own beliefs, for student criticism can be devastating.

But overly rational teaching has its own limitations. It is hardly applicable to children in the early grades. If, as I have said, teaching is any activity that brings about learning, teaching must be held to include methods other than the purely rational. In the first grade the teacher brings about the kind of learning a pupil needs at that age—socialization, perhaps, or acculturation, or good habit formation. When a first-grade child asks why he has been requested to do such and such, he does not expect to receive a highly rational reply. All he wants is an answer that he can understand, one that satisfies his curiosity or his need for attention. The world of the child in the early grades is lively, animated, and imaginative, hardly a world dominated by reason.

Thus teaching is not simply the activity of deliberately inculcating habits, norms, information, and skills, even if we take into account the condition that what has been taught must be remembered. Some inculcation there must be, even some indoctrination, as against the evils of rape, venereal disease, and

---

[16] I do not refer here to the so-called "neutrality" of science or the "objectivity" of factual knowledge. Certainly there can be no argument about many scientific and empirical facts, laws, and theories. I refer to the act of teaching and to the attitudes of teachers with respect to what they are teaching. I can teach Communism or Presbyterianism or the phlogiston theory objectively and didactically. But I would hardly be expected (and perhaps not allowed) to indoctrinate my class into a belief in them.

child abandonment, and for the goods of promise fulfillment, integrity, and physical health. Teaching is good when the method of teaching is adapted to the kind of learning desired. Good teaching involves submitting subject matter to the independent judgment of students wherever it is suitable to do so. It also involves sorting out the various elements in this subject matter. In science, for example, we may teach (a) the straightforward facts of science, (b) the meaning of science (personal, social, epistemological, etc.), (c) the value of science, (d) how to think scientifically, and (e) how to solve problems in science. The good science teacher attends to all these elements. He knows which is which, how they are to be separated, and how they are to be unified.

The teacher also assumes a moral responsibility for the welfare of those in his charge. He is in a position of trust and is therefore likely to be judged severely if he abuses his position. A teacher is one who has a special knowledge of his subject and his pupils. When he is licensed or given a certificate, he does not simply go out and teach; he is morally obligated to teach well. He has accepted quite explicitly the responsibility to see that learning does indeed take place. Of course, no teacher can *guarantee* that learning will take place. He can encourage, even cajole, a pupil into learning, but he cannot in the long run *make* him learn. Only the pupil can do that for himself.

This means that control by the teacher, teacher authority, must be recognized as a necessary prerogative of teaching. A teacher is an authority not only with respect to his subject matter but also with respect to the classes he teaches. Some teachers, especially beginners, are fearful of losing the affection of their pupils, so they hesitate to use this authority. But a teacher's authority comes to him whether he wants it or not by virtue of his professional role. Parents and pupils *expect* him to be an authority, and pupils know they are in school to learn from him.

The teacher then, like the British householder, is king of his castle, with all the rights, privileges, and responsibilities that go with it. One of his rights is to be obeyed by those over whom he has authority. To secure obedience he may even use force or delegate its use. This is quite proper, for unless authority can have recourse to force, it may be flouted at will. Of course the teacher must exercise his authority wisely and responsibly. He must also remember that his authority is less than that of a parent. The teacher-pupil relationship may be affectionate, but it does not involve parental love and devotion. It is essentially temporary and limited: temporary in that a teacher does not normally teach a particular child more than a year or two, limited in that the learning that the teacher directs is, or should be, primarily intellectual. It is a relationship determined ultimately by the principles of a very old profession.

CONCEPT OF EQUALITY

Now let us take the concept of equality. In this country belief in equality is so strong that the traditional policy of "separate but equal" schools for nonwhites is no longer officially accepted. In the name of equal educational opportunity the doors of most institutions of higher education are open to all secondary-school graduates. Everyone, it is said, has a right to attend school or college up to a point of obviously diminishing returns.[17]

Nevertheless, there is little agreement on what we mean by "equality" or "equal treatment." My dictionary states that "equal" means alike or same in quantity, degree, value, ability, etc. It gives other definitions too, such as "not having sufficient power or ability," as in the expression, "He was not equal to the task." For the moment, however, let us confine our atten-

---

[17] Over the last decade the concept of equality has been much discussed by educational philosophers. Even though one essay is entitled "Too Much Equality" (B. Paul Komisar and Jerrold R. Coombs, *Studies in Philosophy and Education*, Fall 1965, 263 ff.), it is certain that other authors will assert that we do not have enough. Perhaps the most engaging contribution is Paul Nash's "Two Cheers for Equality," in *Teachers College Record* (December 1965), pp. 217 ff.

tion to the first meaning, that of "likeness" or "sameness."

In the sense of sameness in degree or quantity, the term "equality" gives us no trouble. When we say, "John's IQ is equal to Mary's," we know that if John's IQ is 110 Mary's is 110 too. But what do we mean when we say, "The teacher gave equal treatment to John and Mary"? Do we imply that the teacher spent the same amount of time with each? That if he kept John after school he kept Mary too? That despite their different personalities he handled both pupils exactly alike? Obviously there is something puzzling about using "equal" in the sense of "same."

Perhaps there are times when we should give pupils *unequal* treatment. Surely Mary should not be kept after school just because John is. Yet if I said, "The teacher gave John and Mary unequal treatment," I would seem to be accusing the teacher of discrimination. "Equal," we see, is a word that usually connotes something fine and desirable. Human beings, it is said, are "born free and equal." People who think that men are not born this way are regarded as uncivilized. We may, it is true, remember the parable of the talents, which makes the point that some people, as a result of birth or environment, are more talented than others. But at least, we say, all people should be *treated* as equals. They should all have an equal *opportunity*, an equal chance, to make the best of whatever talents they possess.

But this only compounds the difficulty, for opportunity is not something that can be quantified into a measure for you and the same measure for me. And what is an opportunity for me may not be an opportunity for you. How then can any opportunity or chance be equal? Indeed, we may first have to provide equality, whatever that is, before we can provide opportunity. Obviously, even when all children have "equal opportunity" to attend school, those children who are significantly disadvantaged will have less chance of succeeding in school than those who are not. Suppose we then do what we can to bring the disadvantaged to the same starting line as the advantaged. Do we not now fall into the trap of treating unequally those who already are at the starting line? A teacher has only so much time and energy. If in a class of 30 he concentrates on the disadvantaged, others in the class will be neglected. We live, let us remember, in a highly competitive society. Cooperation is a fine ideal, but if we want to get ahead (and who does not?), we must also compete. Even the finest minds need guidance and challenge, and students possessing such minds are in school for that purpose. Are we not, then, just as well off omitting "equal" before opportunity? The adjective seems both redundant and confusing. The best we can surely do is to provide an opportunity—equal or not—for everyone to get the kind of education to which he is *justifiably* entitled, about which more will be said in a moment.

To recapitulate, it seems that when we employ the term "equality" to mean "sameness," we not only use it narrowly but we also actually negate its dictionary meaning. We say that treating people equally means treating them the same, yet we find that in order to be fair to the disadvantaged we must treat them differently, that is, not the same, unequally. If Mary comes from a disadvantaged home and John comes from a comfortable middle-class home, the teacher is not as a rule expected to treat them equally but rather unequally in order to bring about a greater equality (social, economic, vocational, etc.) between them. This is the whole point of compensatory education.

Let us try a second approach, one that the alert reader may already have considered. If we say that the teacher treated Mary and John equally, perhaps what we really mean is that he treated them *justly,* or *fairly,* or *fittingly.* The teacher kept John after school, but it was not fair (or fitting) for him to treat Mary in the same way because Mary had not misbehaved like John. No trouble here. Now suppose I say, "The teacher gave equal treatment to both sides of an issue." This seems praiseworthy enough, for in a truly democratic society teachers are expected to do just this. But what does this equal treatment entail? That the teacher devotes twenty minutes to each side? That the teacher presents six arguments for and half a dozen against? That the teacher spends five minutes in turn describing, explaining, advocating, refuting one side and then five minutes doing the same with the other? Hardly. For one thing, the teacher may not need to explain one side because the students already have studied that side themselves. They may indeed have studied it so well that the teacher can devote all his time to the other side. At first reading this may sound pointless, but it is only a *reductio ad absurdum* of the way some people use the term "equality."

Since we cannot afford to be pointless, let us try a third approach. Why not let the student himself decide what equal treatment is? Why not ask the student what he understands by equal treatment and whether he is getting it? In this case, however, we assume that the student can *justify* his claim. It is no use just letting him sound off. Here, then, the student needs knowledge about justifying moral claims in general and his claim of equality in particular. There are some justifying principles that he may take from ethics. He might, for example, refer to Kant's categorical imperative, that we should act "only on that maxim which we can at the same time will to be a universal law." This imperative represents Kant's classic principle of impartiality and respect for persons, that no one shall demand favored treatment unless he can advance good reasons for it. In other words, we are obligated to treat people "equally" (that is, the same) until we have good cause to treat them differently. Obviously, if a student were disadvantaged in some understandable way, we would be justified in giving him different treatment. He is not an equal and therefore should not be treated equally.

So we return to such notions as justice, fairness, and fittingness. After all, when people demand equality, what they really want is justice, fair play, and treatment appropriate to their needs. But what makes our reasons good? We know that shrewd people can produce seemingly good reasons for what appear to be quite blatant acts of inequality. To this I reply that our reasons must be (a) relevant, (b) socially viable, and (c) defensible. *Relevance* best can be established by appealing to sound ethical principles. I could justify a statement that it is wrong to treat people as slaves by citing my ethical beliefs about the dignity of man. In my view slavery is an offense against human dignity. By *social viability* I refer to the possibility of obtaining some particular form of justice within a given society. Obviously, I cannot treat students equally in any sense of the word if law or custom prevents me. My reasons are *defensible* if I have reached them logically and if they are grounded in an ethical theory that I can rationally demonstrate to be beneficial to mankind. Now of course there may be some argument over whether my reasons are better than yours or whether I have proved my case. If so, we may have to have recourse to courts of law. The Supreme Court is a last resort when disputes have to be settled, and although the justices themselves in turn become disputants, majority opinion even here in the end prevails.

How comforting to be able to rely on the Supreme Court for answers! The settlement, however, is chiefly a legal one, and in reaching it the justices too have had to educate themselves. They have had to appeal to ethical principles, to philosophies of law and human conduct. Even so, very few cases involving equality actually reach the Supreme Court. Most of them have to be settled in the arena of education where the challenge is issued. Schooling is an urgent matter. Teachers cannot wait; emergencies arise every hour; decisions must be made on the spot. The teacher must have reflected on questions of equality and must be ready to draw on his fund of ethical knowledge.

CONCLUSION

There is no doubt that analysis has improved educational philosophy, making it more rigorous and also more sensitive to the manifold implications of educational terms. On the other hand, analysis alone is incomplete as a philosophy. It has illuminated individual educational concepts and concept pairs (for example, teaching and learning), but no analytic philosopher has yet sought to coordinate or systematize major educational concepts. In time analysts may undertake such systematizing; to date they have shown no taste for it.

Education is the conscious molding of man by men. It rests

on conceptions of man and society that can be judged only by an educational philosophy that embraces the full range of philosophy's subject matter. Analysis has not invalidated this concern but rather has turned away from it. Thus the influence of analysis on present-day educational philosophy should not lead us to conclude that the other functions of educational philosophy, the speculative and the prescriptive, have been superseded. They have not. They are needed now as much as they have ever been.

References

There are two major systematic studies of logic in education: my own *Logic and Language of Education* (Wiley, 1966, 242 pp.), and Robert H. Ennis' *Logic in Teaching* (Prentice-Hall, 1969, 520 pp.). B. Othanel Smith and his associates have published several studies on aspects of logic in teaching, such as *A Study of the Strategies of Teaching* (Bureau of Educational Research, University of Illinois, 1967) and *A Study of the Logic of Teaching* (Bureau of Educational Research, University of Illinois, n.d.).

On philosophic analysis in general I recommend John Hospers, *An Introduction to Philosophical Analysis* (Prentice-Hall, 1965). On logic and analysis with reference to education, see D. J. O'Connor, *An Introduction to the Philosophy of Education* (Routledge and Kegan Paul, London, 1957), and L. M. Brown, *General Philosophy in Education* (McGraw-Hill, 1966, 244 pp.), which is well equipped with exercises and discussion questions. In the field of language analysis Israel Scheffler's *The Language of Education* (Charles C Thomas, Springfield, Illinois, 1960, 113 pp.) opened the way for other works, such as Jonas P. Soltis, *An Introduction to the Analysis of Educational Concepts* (Addison-Wesley, 1968, 100 pp.), James Gribble, *Introduction to Philosophy of Education* (Allyn and Bacon, 1969, 198 pp.), and Glenn Langford, *Philosophy and Education* (Macmillan, London, 1969, 160 pp.). Like Soltis, Gribble and Langford focus entirely on the analysis of language and concepts in education. They do not consider other modes of philosophy. Beginning students may find Soltis the most readable. Gribble, influenced by R. S. Peters, is incisive. Langford brings analysis closer to the classroom.

Index